YOUR NEXT THIRTY DAYS OF RELATIONSHIPS

DEAN FULKS

& Writers from Lifepoint Church

Printed in the United States of America

All Scriptures taken from The Holy Bible, English Standard
Version unless otherwise noted.

Published by Author Academy Elite
P.O. Box 43, Powell, OH 43035
www.AuthorAcademyElite.com

Paperback ISBN-13: 978-1-64085-534-2
Ebook ISBN-13: 978-1-64085-535-9

Library of Congress Control Number: 2018968543

Available in softcover, e-book, and audiobook.

CONTENTS

Day 1 – Love First – Dean F.   1
         Why Your "Self" Should Come Second

Day 2 – The Marriage Covenant
         – Brad & Kati L.   7
         A Leisurely Stroll into Death

Day 3 – God's Strategy Behind Matrimony
         – Kale B.   14
         How the Why Can Repair the What

Day 4 – Kings and Queens – Chris J.   21
         Waiting for the One You Want

Day 5 – In Sickness and in Health
         – Scott R.   30
         *How Chronic Illness Affects Your
         Affections*

Day 6 – A War of Words – Ray G.   37
         *Why You Should Overemphasize
         Understanding*

Day 7 – God Created Women and Sex
         – Meredith D.   44
         *Why Christians Should Talk More
         about Both*

Day 8 – Just Call on Me, Brother – Gail H.   52
         Navigating the Single Life

Day 9 – When Type A Marries Type B
– Allison M.   59
*How to Preach the Gospel into
Your Marriage*

Day 10 – Marriage and Money – Brad C.   65
*How to Keep Finances from
Causing Fights*

Day 11 – Working through a Marriage Crisis
– Derek & Rachel H.   73
Finding the Upside of Down

Day 12 – Basic Training
– Brendan & Kristy N.   81
*Why Discipleship is Man's
Best Friend*

Day 13 – Relationships, Anxiety,
& Depression – Ryan B.   89
Finding Light in the Darkness

Day 14 – History Class – Heather T.   97
Getting Past Your Past

Day 15 – Sex & Men – Mike D.   103
*How Divinity, Masculinity, and
Sexuality Work Together*

Day 16 – The Knock on Your Door that
No One Wants to Answer
– Darwin & Stephanie M.   111
God & Grieving

Day 17 – Just Say So – Cindy & Bryan M. 118
*How to Trust God to Speak Truth
into Your Relationship*

Day 18 – Dealing with Divorce – Louise B. 124
*What to Do When You
Don't Know What to Do*

Day 19 – Going Forwards Backwards
– Linda & John H. 130
How God Can Restore Relationships

Day 20 – Imperfectly Perfect – Rachelle A. 136
*When Super-Christians Learn
Surrender*

Day 21 – Stirring the Right Stuff
– Shane & Ellen T. 144
*Modern Day Experiences
for Old School Values*

Day 22 – When Your Child Hurts
– Carrie H. 151
*Learning to Give Thanks for
It When You Are in It*

Day 23 – Asking Gospel Questions
– Adam P. 159
*How Questions Can Create
Patterns in Our Lives*

Day 24 – Blended Families
– Kevin & Carrie H. 166
Navigating the New Normal

Day 25 – Adoption – Matt & Kristy L.   173
      A Tragically Beautiful Gift

Day 26 – Marriage & Ministry – Ed T.   179
      Opposites Attract

Day 27 – A Peaceful House
      – Steve & Lisa C.   186
      How to Fight Fair

Day 28 – Once a Man, Twice a Child
      – John & Jenifer W.   193
      Caring for Aging Parents

Day 29 – Marriage & Mission
      – Brian & Heidi F.   200
      Loving Each Other
      to Love the World

Day 30 – Work-Life Balance – Kary O.   207
      How to Do the Most Important
      Things without Burning Out

Appendix – "Everyday" – Lisa C.   215

A NOTE TO THE READER

Just Google "the most important word in the Bible."
There are LOTS of opinions.

I think most Christians would say "Jesus," right?
Some argue that His name is the most important
word in the Bible. But if we're just considering words
and not taking names into account, then let's throw
it out for debate…what's the most important **word**
in the Bible?

There are lots of great words. Salvation.
Redemption. Resurrection. Grace. Hope. Mercy.
Love. Peace. The list is endless.

But what if the most important word in the Bible
is NOT even in the Bible?

The first Christian book that I read outside of the
Bible was called *The Concentric Circles of Concern*.
The author was Oscar Thompson, and he suggested
that the most important, non-personal word in the
most important book ever written wasn't even in
the Book.

The word is relationships. The Bible is a book about relationships from cover to cover—our relationship with God and our relationships with each other.

This is also a relationship book...but a different sort. I asked twenty-nine different people/couples to write this book with me. Twenty-nine different perspectives on relationships litter the pages of this book. Cohesiveness probably won't be our strength. However, each day ends with a practical idea and some lines to write out applications or prayers. Please use them.

I am blessed to personally know these authors, their stories, and their lives. Their wisdom, perspective, and stories will make you laugh, cry, and hopefully think about your Creator.

Hopefully, you won't just think about your Creator—we hope that you think towards Him.

Whether you are single, engaged, married, or parenting, we hope that these next thirty days will change your relationships...that you will sense that you have a place to belong and become all that God intends.

Dean Fulks & Lifepoint Writers

DAY 1
LOVE FIRST

Why Your "Self" Should Come Second

– Dean F.

We have four rules in our family. As a matter of fact, we refer to them as the "Fulks Family Rules." Some of these I've picked up and some were my own invention.

Fulks Family Rule #1 – "God first, family second." (I'm a pastor, so I have to start with that one)

Fulks Family Rule #2 – "Life is not fair." (Thanks to my big brother for the help on that one)

Fulks Family Rule #3 – "There are no amendments to rule #2."

Fulks Family Rule #4 – "Fulks never quit."

That's us…four basic rules. I don't think I've ever run those through a theological grid, but I have repeated them to my kids for years. And as I gain some perspective, I wish I would've added Rule #5: "Relationships are not easy."

Today, some would suggest that humans are nothing more than a cocktail of tissues, hormones, and chemicals. In other words, we are just animals. At the other end of the spectrum, because churches don't often talk about the difficult aspects of relationships, it's almost like we're angels.

We are neither animals nor angels.

We are humans created to reflect the glory of God. In fact, we are the only part of God's creation that has both a body and a soul. So, while we must navigate our tissues, hormones, and chemicals in relation to others, we also have a soul that relates to God. It's wonderful at times, handling these different relationships, but it's rarely easy.

God not only created humans to be relational, but He exists in community, as well. From the beginning, we see a relational God who loves us in spite of our flaws. And He's not only relational with us, but He also exists in the community of the Trinity. We see this in Genesis 1:26 when God said, "Let us make man in our image, after our likeness." For us, family may be the best example we have of this godly principle of living in community.

When our oldest daughter, Sydney, turned ten-years-old, she got a gift card to a store called Justice, and she wanted to use it to buy a new shirt. At that time in our lives, we were planting a church, had three kids, and were a hand-me-down kind of home. So, getting a new shirt was a big deal. Sylvia, our youngest daughter, was around five at that time, and she thought she should get a new shirt, as well. Actually, Sylvia was determined to get a new shirt. Angie offered to get Sylvia a shirt off of the clearance rack. However, that was not enough for our five-year-old fashionista!

When Sylvia didn't get what she wanted, she threw a fit…she screamed, cried, and threw herself on the ground. And all of the other moms were giving Angie the eye roll that said, "She ought to discipline that kid." "Oh, I think that's the pastor's wife." "Well, that explains everything." Actually, I'm sure no one really thought any of those things, but it felt that way to an anxious young mom.

Sylvia left without a shirt. Instead, she was taken out of the store and put into her car seat. Our five-year-old was then cry-heaving (not dry-heaving—if you've been there, you know), and Angie said, "I cannot believe you acted like that… crying and throwing a fit." Suddenly, Sylvia stopped crying to say, "Well, I wouldn't have had to act that way if you'd just bought me that shirt." Uh-oh…justice was about to be served in the Justice parking lot!

Angie later demonstrated this voice that came out of her. She called it deep; I called it demonic (but of course, I didn't say that). She said to Sylvia, "Don't you dare blame your disobedience on me… wait 'til we get home." To which Sylvia responded, "I want Dad!"

When Angie shared the story with me, my immediate thought was, "Don't bring me into this, kid!"

In the end, Angie and Sylvia worked through the situation at home because family means that we love each other, even when we don't always like each other. Fulks Family Rule #1 was at work. But why do we love our families that way?

1 John 4:19 – *We love because he first loved us.*

I've often thought about how I must appear to God just as Sylvia looked to Angie on that day. By the way, Sylvia is a great kid, but she learned a big lesson on that shopping trip—a lesson I feel like I learn again and again.

Day 1 Key Concept: Your "self" should come second

Just as Sylvia couldn't understand that Angie, her parent, knew that she didn't need a shirt, I also throw fits in front of God when I don't get my way. "But, God, other people are getting these blessings… what about me?" "I'm a church planter. I DESERVE these things."

I love that God loves me anyway. On the days I feel God doesn't like me very much (I don't think I can prove that theologically), He still loves me. And I can prove that in the person of Christ. The Gospel means I don't get judgment from God. Instead, I receive forgiveness and get to be with my eternal Father, my Dad. Why don't I get justice for my misbehavior? Because Jesus took my just punishment and granted me freedom—freedom to love people without laying heavy expectations on them. I have the liberty to love others as God's creation and put them into His hands.

Remember, we're not animals who have to self-protect and seek revenge. Neither are we angels who exist in perfect harmony. We are the created children of a loving Heavenly Father who gives us freedom. We imperfectly reflect His glory. Life is not fair, which is actually good for you. You and I don't get what our actions deserve. Why?

Because. God. Never. Ever. Ever. Quits. Loving. You.

A Next Step:

Putting ourselves second is both a beautiful part of the Great Commission and a difficult part of our struggle with brokenness. Take time to pray today and ask God what part(s) of you needs to be moved out of first place, as you begin this thirty-day journey. Use the lines below to write them down.

_____

_____

_____

_____

_____

_____

_____

_____

_____

_____

_____

_____

_____

_____

_____

_____

_____

_____

_____

_____

_____

_____

_____

_____

_____

_____

_____

_____

_____

_____

_____

_____

_____

_____

DAY 2
THE MARRIAGE COVENANT

A Leisurely Stroll into Death

– Brad & Kati L.

Fifteen years ago my wife, Kati, and I were married in our hometown of Bossier City, Louisiana. Today we live in Fort Smith, Arkansas and have three children and a dog! Life is pretty good. However, like most, Kati and I navigate the difficulties of marriage and family daily. I once heard this question asked, "Do you know what you get when two sinners get married? One big sinner!" That is so true, at least in our case.

As Kati and I reflect on our early struggles, we can now laugh about them. But in those early moments, marriage was very difficult. Kati was raised to make her bed...I was not (on one occasion she actually made the bed with me in it!). I left my shoes in living room floor to be picked up later...Kati put her shoes away immediately. I liked to eat junk food... Kati was very health-conscious. I liked television... Kati liked to talk. We even argued differently. The truth is all of those differences can be a recipe for disaster if not filtered through the lens of the One who created man and woman and designed them to be united in marriage.

There is no question that marriage can be difficult. And if the statistics are right, every first time marriage has a 50% chance of lasting—not great odds! Imagine if on your wedding day, you looked at your husband or wife and said, "Honey, I hope we make it!" But the truth is, that's statistically how most marriages start.

One of the most important questions we should be asking is, what must we do in order to make our marriages last? Kati and I would like to suggest two truths to consider for the health and longevity of your marriage.

1. We must die.

Every wedding ceremony should begin with those words because that's what it means to enter into a covenant—and marriage was always meant to be a covenant. If there's one thing that will kill a marriage, it's selfishness.

What exactly is a covenant? Merriam-Webster defines a covenant as, "a usually formal, solemn, and binding agreement." When God made a covenant with His people, He designed it to have eternal and lasting implications, and His people in the Old Testament took covenants very seriously.

In fact, the Old Testament covenant ceremony involved a "walk of death," which constitutes the core issue of the covenant. An animal was killed and split down the middle. The covenant participants would walk in a figure eight between the halves of the animal, reciting the duties of the covenant, and returning to face each other. The figure eight, a symbol of eternity, was an acknowledgement that the covenant was forever. This covenantal "walk of death" said one important thing: I am dying to myself and giving up the rights to my individual life to become one with my covenant partner. THAT is what God intended when he officiated the first wedding.

And right from the beginning, we see that Adam and Eve were made to be in covenant with each other; they were made to be one:

Genesis 2:22-24 – *And the rib that the LORD God had taken from the man he made into a woman and brought her to the man. Then the man said, "This at last is bone of my bones and flesh of my flesh; she shall be call Woman, because she was taken out of Man." Therefore a man shall leave his father and his mother and hold fast to his wife, and they shall become one flesh.*

Notice the description of this event in the text:

"Bone of my bones"
"Flesh of my flesh"
"One flesh"

This is the core of a covenant marriage—oneness. When you see your marriage relationship as "two becoming one," the game changes.

"I" is transformed to "US"
"Me" changes to "WE"

This sentiment of oneness is also implied in Song of Solomon 2:16: "My beloved is mine, and I am his...."

So, what's the takeaway? Selflessness is the key to any successful marriage. Still, as Christians, our marriages are meant to accomplish more than simply fulfilling each other's physical needs or raising a family. This brings us to the second truth.

2. We are a reflection.

Marriage is not an earthly creation of man, but it was designed by God to reflect Jesus' covenantal relationship with His church. We see this true purpose of marriage in Ephesians:

Ephesians 5:31-32 – *"Therefore a man shall leave his father and mother and hold fast to his wife, and the two shall become one flesh." This mystery is profound, and I am saying that it refers to Christ and the church.*

In other words, our covenant with our spouse is meant to reflect God's eternal, everlasting covenant with us. So, marriage is so much more than an earthly relationship. It's a mirror that reflects eternal realities. Therefore, the highest meaning and ultimate purpose of marriage is to put the covenant relationship of Christ and his church on display for the world to see.

Day 2 Key Concept: Marriage exists to reflect Jesus' covenant with his church

So, every time a couple "ties the knot," they are making a death march, of sorts. However, God never wastes anything. Just like in nature, death leads to life, and the same is true in marriage. When "me" becomes "we" and "I" becomes "us," you are fully alive to reflect God's glory in a new way.

However, I want to we, when it's convenient for me. What I really want is a consumer marriage. More service at a lower price. I want the discounted version of marriage…the one on the clearance rack, where I get something good that doesn't cost me as much.

The problem is obvious. Reflecting Christ means that I must reflect His sacrifice, as much as humanly possible. Our spouses should see and sense that. Think of the glory given to God when two people willingly submit their desires to each other in the same way that Jesus submitted Himself to the Cross on our behalf. It doesn't get much better than that!

A Next Step:

Differences reveal our need for humility. If you are single, what areas do you tend to struggle with in relationships? If you are in a long-term relationship, simply having a conversation about the reality that your way isn't always the "right way" can be an act of humility. Set a time for that conversation.

_____

_____

_____

_____

_____

_____

_____

_____

_____

_____

_____

_____

_____

_____

_____

_____

_____

_____

DAY 3
GOD'S STRATEGY BEHIND MATRIMONY

How the Why Can Repair the What

– Kale B.

When I think about the past few years of my life, I often oscillate between a range of emotions…sheer gratitude, exhaustion, wonder, feelings of being overwhelmed, and laughter at God's timing. Let me offer a brief timeline:

October 2014 – Get engaged to my lovely wife, Morgan
December 2014 – Morgan graduates from college
February 2015 – Get married
April 2015 – Find out we're pregnant (Surprise!)
June 2015 – Move from Mount Vernon to Delaware

October 2015 – Officially transition from College/Youth
Pastor to Teaching Pastor/Church Planter
January 2016 – First baby, Cade, arrives
March 2016 – Delaware campus of Lifepoint Church
officially launches
June 2016 – We move again (within Delaware city, at
least!)
July 2016 – We find out we're pregnant with baby #2
(Surprise again!)
April 2017 – Second baby, Lleyton, arrives

Yep.

I chuckle because experienced people tell you to
avoid making "major life changes" in the beginning
years of marriage. It's hard to imagine Morgan and
I violating that more than we did, except for maybe
buying a puppy. We did buy a kitten shortly after
marriage (but that was so traumatizing I don't really
want to talk about it).

It would be fun to say that things have begun
to slow down, but there's a word for that—lying.
At the time of writing this, we're in the middle of
renovating a new space for our church and expecting
baby #3. Now, hear me say this loud and clear—all
of the things that I'm writing about are wonderful
things. Children, a new job, moving to a great town,
a growing church—these are blessings! Morgan and
I really do thank the Lord for giving us so much
more than we could ask for, deserve, or imagine.

At the same time, this crazy pace, coupled with
the blending of two very different (and sinful)
people, has caused tension, stress, and miscommu-
nication in our marriage that took both of us by

surprise. Shortly before we got married, I actually remember telling my soon-to-be wife that, when it came to my temper, I "had a pretty long fuse" and it was "pretty difficult to get under my skin." Turns out, I was an idiot.

Neither of us anticipated arguments that lasted until the late hours of the night. Neither of us expected having to work so hard to make sure the other person understood what we meant by a certain look or phrase. I never thought I would see my wife crying in the corner of the closet, because she was so overwhelmed. She probably never expected to see me so frustrated and angry that I didn't even know how to talk about it (I talk about pretty much everything, so seeing me at a loss for words is a little bit like seeing a unicorn.)

Now, I'm not saying we have a bad marriage. Quite the opposite. I think we have a really healthy marriage, and Morgan would say the same. But part of the reason we can say that—and mean it—is because we've begun to understand that God defines "healthy" in a marriage differently than our world does. That's because God defines the purpose of marriage differently than our culture.

Look briefly with me at this passage from Scripture:

1 Corinthians 13:4-8 – *Love is patient, love is kind. It does not envy, it does not boast, it is not proud. It does not dishonor others, it is not self-seeking, it is not easily angered, it keeps no record of wrongs. Love does not delight in evil but rejoices with the truth. It always protects, always trusts, always hopes, always perseveres. Love never fails. (NIV)*

Most of us have heard this read so many times at weddings that, quite possibly, we've glossed over it and haven't actually heard or thought about what it says. Look at some of those descriptions about what it means to love: patience, kindness, humility, selflessness, not easily angered, always perseveres....

Here's something really crazy—Paul, the author, isn't even talking about marriage. He's talking about how Christians should love one another, married or not...let that one sink in for a moment.

Now, back to the purpose of marriage. Within the covenant relationship of marriage, you get a chance to live out what Paul is talking about in the closest, most intimate human relationship a person can have. There's just one problem—in our own strength, none of us can do that well!

And you know what? Marriage shows us that. You see, in God's hands, marriage can be like a mirror. We look into it, and we see how sinful we are. It becomes so clear how short we fall of God's standard for how we should love and serve our spouse.

What I quickly (and painfully) discovered in just a short time of marriage is that I'm not always patient, kind, or selfless. In fact, far too often I am short-tempered, harsh, and selfish. I want my way, I want Morgan to serve me, and I often look to her to make my life easier rather than seeking to love and serve her well. When things go wrong, I don't always trust or persevere or protect. Instead, it's easy to blame her and her issues rather than running to God for me and my issues.

So what are we supposed to do with all of this? What do we do when we are painfully exposed to our brokenness?

We ask for God's forgiveness, thank Him for Jesus and the Cross, and ask for His help.

And that brings us to the key concept. We have believed the lie that marriage's primary purpose is to make us happy. However, Scripture shows us that God uses marriage to make us holy (in other words, to make us more like Jesus).

Day 3 Key Concept: God uses marriage to make us holy

Marriage—as an institution—is not designed to complete us, improve our lives, and make all of our dreams come true. However, if you've seen a romantic comedy, then you know what the culture says about how marriage works: You find your "soul mate," everything pretty much falls into line, and your marriage just "works." You ride off together into the horizon and experience the "happily ever after" that every Disney movie since the beginning of time talks about…by the way, you won't find the term or even the concept of a "soul mate" anywhere in the Bible.

Finding your "happily ever after" isn't the point. I'm not saying you shouldn't be happy in your marriage. I'm saying that happiness is a by-product of holiness. As God, by His Spirit, shapes you and your spouse to be more like Jesus, happiness is something that emerges. In the end, God's desire for your life and your marriage is that they glorify Him and point others to Him. That happens as you and your spouse become more and more like Jesus through both the wonderful and difficult moments of marriage.

A Next Step:

Marriage is one way that grows our hearts for Him. Identify an area today that you can sense God is using in your marriage to sanctify you. Share that with your spouse and also an area that you can see God's activity in your spouse. If you are single, do the same thing with a friend whom you trust.

_____
_____
_____
_____
_____
_____
_____
_____
_____
_____
_____
_____

_____

_____

_____

_____

_____

_____

_____

_____

_____

_____

_____

_____

_____

_____

_____

_____

_____

_____

_____

_____

_____

_____

_____

_____

_____

DAY 4
KINGS AND QUEENS

Waiting for the One You Want

– Chris J.

"An excellent wife who can find? She is far more precious than jewels. The heart of her husband trusts in her, and he will have no lack of gain. She does him good, and not harm, all the days of her life." Proverbs 31:10-12

I recall being a young college grad and hanging out with other single guys at our Athletes in Action summer ministry training in sunny Ft. Collins, Colorado. We all had dating and marriage on our minds. The issue was magnified because Campus Crusade for Crusade (now known as Cru) had brought a large contingent of single girls to the same training location.

For some reason, that amazing Bible training felt, at times, like a distraction to my youthful hormones. There were literally hundreds of eligible women everywhere. I felt like an overwhelmed little kid who was placed in a Toys R Us and given $1,000 to spend.

I ended up learning some important lessons that summer...

#1. "If you want to marry a Queen, you have to become a King."

Author and speaker Josh McDowell said this (he happened to be one of my summer instructors). His statement changed my thinking and set me free. I started to focus on growing as a person instead of focusing on landing the most prized woman before the other dudes snared her first. The stress of the race subsided, and I could move on to developing my faith and aims in life.

<u>Guys</u> – Focus on your relationship with God, your personal growth, how to give back to others, and the career path that make all these work together for you. Merely keep your eyes open to a potential mate, as opposed to "hunting one down."

<u>Gals</u> – Though it is very flattering to be desired, focus on knowing God in an intimate way and finding security in confidential talks with Him first. Keep your eyes open to qualities you like in the men you meet and know, but patiently become dependent

on Christ. If you think a man is going to meet all your needs, then you are in for a very frustrating marriage.

#2. Changing your focus changes your life

When I changed my focus that summer, I found more ladies were interested in me than when I was just pursuing them. I discovered that gals are more attracted to a guy who is "going somewhere" in his life, as opposed to the fella who is totally focused on her.

Confession time—my whole family comes to our house to watch *The Bachelor* or *The Bachelorette* every week. The ladies are intrigued by the drama, and the guys enjoy comically abusing the contestants. One finale came down to two men with different approaches. One was NFL star quarterback Aaron Rogers' brother who had career direction and goals, which meant Miss Bachelorette would have to move from her hometown for him. Conversely, the other bachelor proclaimed he would do anything for her… give up his dreams, his home, blah blah blah…if she picked him. Sounded romantic, but boom—dumped! She picked Rogers, the guy who was willing to lose her because he found, in a sense, his direction in life and was asking her to get on board and join him in that journey.

<u>Guys</u> – As you pursue "becoming a King," keep your eyes open for women who have common interests, who understand your direction, and who you could see as a teammate in life, instead of just a

beautiful conquest. Is she someone you could work well with in life?

Gals – As you grow as a "Queen," think about a lifetime of connection instead of just finding someone who gives you status or someone who will meet all your needs (Trust me. That guy is not out there. There are mirages, but please don't bank on somebody completely fulfilling you). Is he someone you could work well with in life?

#3. Be realistic about what marriage is

Ron Ralston, a speaker for Campus Crusade, also had a major impact on my life that summer. He pointed out that a husband and wife spend merely a fraction of a percent of their time in actual physical intimacy. In spite of that fact, while looking for a spouse, we tend to base a lot on physical appearance and intimacy.

While I believe there needs to be physical attraction, respect and camaraderie are also paramount in finding a marriage partner. When couples say they need to find out if they are physically compatible, it makes me chuckle. There is no question that God has made men and women physically compatible. That's not the issue. The interpersonal stuff is what makes a relationship fulfilling.

Here's where most young dating couples blow it. They get too physical and have a difficult time truly knowing the person they are dating. I'm convinced that physical intimacy blurs the picture. It's like trying to have an important conversation with a poor cell phone connection.

Becoming too physical turns a good relationship into a stressful one, and the Christian couple finds themselves doing things that they never intended. The relationship can drag on in guilt, which leads to frustration, bickering, and at best, a weak walk with God (ironically, closeness to God is needed more than ever at this point in a young person's life).

Guys – Respect her. Don't justify following your hormones and the media, who tell you to go for it. Waiting will help you see the other person without the blurry connection. God lovingly set guidelines to protect you and provide for you a wonderful young lady to enjoy in marriage—emotionally, spiritually, and physically. It's worth the wait!

Gals – If he wants to violate your standards, then he doesn't respect you. RUN! Help him keep it clean. Don't feel like you need to compromise to "land a man." If that's what it takes for a certain guy to "like" you, then he's not worth it.

#4. Ask the right questions

My group of summer friends and I were sitting on some old bleachers watching a "yawn festival" of a softball game, when we realized one of the training instructors was sitting next to us. Paul Cox was the pastor of an amazing church in Chicago. He also was an ex-professional baseball player, so we were all extremely intimidated.

I'm always up for a gutsy interaction, so I introduced myself and asked, "So, Pastor Cox, what should we be looking for in a wife?" Not knowing how the burly, middle-aged man of God would respond, we braced ourselves. He looked at us and said, "I don't know why young guys like yourselves don't ask that question more often." There was a corporate sigh of relief that he didn't shoo us away. He then proceeded to drop pearls of wisdom into our eager minds.

He strongly encouraged us to ask questions, as we became interested in a young lady: Do you want to have a career outside the home or live your career as a stay-at-home mom? Do you even want to have kids? Where do you expect to live? What kind of church would you want to attend? How important is income level? Are you interested in pursuing a full-time ministry?

His questions hit me hard. They showed me that marriage is real, and that it's way more than just a crush on an interesting girl (if an emotional crush was the criteria, then I would have been married four times in middle school and ten times in college).

<u>Guys</u> – Ask her questions. Don't interrogate or interview, but do get to know her expectations of life and marriage. If things start to progress toward a possible engagement, don't hesitate to ask the opinion of close friends and family members. We tend to settle because a lot of time hasn't been invested. That's no reason to pursue a marriage. Remember, the biggest enemy to "the best" is "very good."

<u>Gals</u> – Make it a priority to understand where he's coming from and where he's going. Seek the opinion of close friends and family. Being in love with being in love can lead good people to justify bad decisions. Decisions that gratify the "right now" can be extremely painful "later on." My wife, Kelly,

and I have had countless young ladies that we have encouraged and warned, yet they still ignored the stop sign and experienced the crash.

As I think back over that summer and other events of my youth, I can recall a lot of lonely times, a lot of my mistakes that God forgave, a lot of disappointments, a lot of confusion, a lot of fun and adventure, and a lot of good conversations and discoveries. Choosing to stand firm with Christ and place my trust in His faithfulness to provide for me were some of the best choices of my life. I found peace and eventually my wonderful wife of thirty-two years and counting!

Day 4 Key Concept: Being in love with being in love can lead good people to justify bad decisions

A Next Step:

If you are single, take time to think through the heart-level character you are looking for in a long-term partner. Write those in the lines below. Think qualities not qualifications. If you are married, take the opportunity today to encourage your spouse about a character quality you saw early on in your relationship that has proven to be true over time.

_____

_____

_____

_____

_____

_____

_____

_____

_____

_____

_____

_____

_____

_____

_____

_____

_____

DAY 5
IN SICKNESS AND IN HEALTH

How Chronic Illness Affects Your Affections

– Scott R.

There are few days in a person's life that bring more joy than one's wedding day. For many, the planning that goes into making sure the day is special is unlike anything they've ever planned for previously or will ever plan again. The guest list, the photographer, the cake, the honeymoon, and more. Then there's that little part of the ceremony when you publicly make a pledge, a solemn promise to each other, in the presence of guests and God. I remember publicly stating our wedding vows thirty-eight years ago, and I'm pretty sure that during that promise I was thinking about two things: don't mess up the words and when do we leave for our honeymoon?

June 27, 1981. I can clearly remember the last few words of our solemn promises to each other—for richer or poorer, in sickness or health. We were young and already poor, so certainly the poor part wouldn't be an issue. And when it came to health, I thought that couldn't ever possibly be an issue, especially for me. I was the healthiest, most fit guy Kelly Mcgrath could marry.

As a young man, I'd been recruited by most of the major track and field programs across the nation: UCLA, Kansas, Villanova, and of course The Ohio State University. In the months following the summer of 1981, I became a three time Big Ten Champion, ran the fastest 800 meters ever run in the history of The Ohio State University (a record that still stands as of January 1, 2018), earned All American honors twice, and qualified and competed in the 1984 US Olympic Trials. Heck, I even ran for the world famous Santa Monica Track Club where I was a member of a 4x800 meter relay team that ran the tenth fastest time in the history of the world.

Clearly, I was healthy, and at that time, I would've said I would always be healthy. Fast-forward twenty-seven years, and you'll find three children, a thriving business, and a life changing visit to a physician's office.

"Scott, you have Parkinson's disease."

Those were the only words I heard in that thirty-minute appointment. All the planning for our wedding day back in 1981 could not have prepared Kelly or me to hear those words. Suddenly, in mere seconds, the sickness part of our wedding vows was more than just words. Sickness was a reality.

Sure, I had noticed a few changes in my physical abilities, but I knew very little about Parkinson's. Nearly thirteen years later, I can tell you that it isn't just my life that's changed but my entire family's, as well. Kelly, Katie, Jacob, and Emma have all been impacted by my declining health.

Each day presents Kelly with responsibilities similar to that of a mother caring for a toddler: helping me dress, driving me to doctor's appointments, and handling our finances and household maintenance. No longer can she depend on me to handle my share of the load. Obviously this is not the life either of us imagined.

Our children (ages 20, 28 and 30) have experienced life with three different dads, even though all three have been me. The older two were raised by Scott the fun, vibrant, happy, healthy dad who had the ability to provide and care for their needs. They were away at college when this life-changing health event really began to impact our home life. Emma, on the other hand, has seen up close the changes in my personality and physical abilities. And she's experienced life with a father who, in many ways, is much older than his chronological age. All three have witnessed their mom in the caregiver role.

The emotional aspect of this journey is overwhelming. I am dependent on Kelly, and she has a new set of responsibilities that quite frankly are emotionally and physically exhausting. I was supposed to be the physically strong person in our marriage, and now at times, I deal with feelings of guilt. I have a disease that worsens, and this new way of life can be nothing short of depressing. Kelly and I haven't switched roles; instead my diminished abilities have increased Kelly's daily responsibilities. Honestly, it would be easier for her to walk away from our marriage, and there is a part of me that, at times, would understand if she did. But what keeps us going is our shared faith in something bigger than Parkinson's and all of the issues and nonreversible changes that come with it. We have faith in Jesus Christ.

Don't get me wrong. Life with Parkinson's isn't easy because we are Christians. In fact, I think faith is easy to talk about when everything is going well. However, after being diagnosed, I knew what it really meant to accept God's will, when the sickness and health part of my wedding vows became a reality.

Now, what? My wife, Kelly, didn't sign up for this future. Come to think of it, we actually did on June 27, 1981. Our wedding vows were a promise to each other in the presence of our Lord and Savior, Jesus Christ. And thankfully, that seventeen-year-old girl who used to ask me if I was "saved" when we started dating way back in 1976 is caring for me in sickness. I am so thankful that Kelly is a follower of Christ, because it is from her relationship with Christ that she draws the strength necessary to be my caregiver.

What else gets us through it? For both of us to know and understand that one day, when we enter the kingdom of Heaven, this sickness will be over is what has allowed us to maintain our relationship and marriage for nearly forty years. To travel this journey without that knowledge would be lonely and depressing. It's interesting how many of us think that this type of thing "only happens to others."

In our case, we are the "others," and we accept and understand that reality without bitterness and the "why us" attitude.

We meant what we promised back in 1981, and thankfully we live by the promises our Lord has made to us. So, why not us?

Revelation 21:1-4 – *Then I saw a new heaven and a new earth, for the first heaven and the first earth had passed away, and the sea was no more. And I saw the holy city, new Jerusalem, coming down out of heaven from God, prepared as a bride adorned for her husband. And I heard a loud voice from the through saying, "Behold, the dwelling place of God is with man. He will dwell with them, and they will be his people, and God himself will be with them as their God. He will wipe away every tear from their eyes, and death shall be no more, neither shall there be mourning, nor crying, nor pain anymore, for the former things have passed away."*

Day 5 Key Concept: Your best day is yet to come

A Next Step:

If you are currently healthy, take the opportunity today to reach out to someone who is going through a health crisis. Find a practical way to meet a need they have. Pray for them. Maybe take the time to write them a card.

_____

_____

_____

_____

_____

_____

_____

_____

_____

_____

_____

_____

_____

_____

_____

_____

_____

_____

_____

_____

_____

DAY 6
A WAR OF WORDS

Why You Should Overemphasize Understanding

– Ray G.

My wife and I went on a date to a great little restaurant. Having a good time catching up, I asked her, "So, how have you been lately?" She began sharing about some struggles she'd been having. And as she talked, the wheels in my head began to turn, "I'm going to fix this for her!" She kept sharing. I began to plan out my thoughts. She was still talking. I carefully designed an outline of the solution. It was perfect. I was sure that what I was about to say was spiritual gold for her. I'd be able to write a sermon about it. When she stopped to take a breath, I launched into my plan. After I finished, I sat a little taller in my seat and was ready for her to crown me

"HUSBAND of the YEAR." She simply said, "Did you even listen to me?" The next two hours went downhill—FAST!

I think we've all felt the effect of poor communication. It can be frustrating and defeating, when we hope for deeper relationships that are stuck on a superficial level. Misunderstandings that have never been resolved can lead to months or years of built up walls and bitterness. Leaders of teams and organizations know they've been plagued by communication breakdowns, when those they lead still don't seem to connect to their heart or vision. And all parents know that poor communication can wreak havoc on their relationships with their children.

We should all take a communication cue from a young Italian, who was born into a wealthy family. This man pursued and enjoyed a life of wealth and pleasure. However, several visions from God led him to turn his life of comfort completely upside down. He ran after the clear mission he'd been given by God—to rebuild His church. As he began his ministry, he asked God to help him by praying, "Grant that I may not so much seek...to be understood, as to understand."

That young Italian eventually became St. Francis of Assisi, and what he prayed is the very heartbeat of what God tells us in Proverbs:

Proverbs 18:2 – *A fool takes no pleasure in understanding, but only in expressing his opinion.*

Day 6 Key Concept: Overemphasize understanding

Leadership guru, Stephen Covey, has this to say about understanding: "If I were to summarize in one sentence the single most important principle I have learned in the field of interpersonal relations, it would be this: Seek first to understand, then to be understood." To "understand" is to uncover the original intent of the message. That is masterful listening!

Masterful listening will affect many areas of life… marriage, family relationships, and our influence in the community are a few. Listening even impacts our health. Dr. James Lynch, co-director of the Psychophysiological Clinic and Laboratories at the University of Maryland, has documented that an actual healing of the cardiovascular system takes place when we "understand." Blood pressure rises when people speak and lowers when they listen. In fact, his studies show that blood pressure is actually lower when people are listening than when they are silently staring at a blank wall. According to Dr. Lynch, "understanding" is essential for good health.

Not only is "understanding" essential for good health and transformed relationships, but it's also the first step towards a relationship with God! Jesus emphasized "understanding" in Mark 4:1-20. In Mark, Jesus tells a parable about four different types of soil interacting with a farmer's seed. The farmer's seed is the Gospel, and the different types of soil describe the different hearts people have to receive the Gospel. The first path doesn't absorb the seed at all. The second, a rocky soil, takes the seed at first but fails to develop roots; it's just a flash in the pan. The third, a thorny soil, allows growth to begin, but worries and other concerns choke it to death. Only the last soil receives the seed and produces much fruit, because the Holy Spirit has opened the heart to understanding.

But why are there different types of soil? Well, look back at our Scripture in Proverbs 18:2: "A fool takes no pleasure in understanding, but only in expressing **his opinion**" (bold mine). There's the culprit! Opinions are like noses—everyone has one.

We've all been given opportunities to listen, but how often do we plug our ears? I grew up with two brothers, and we basically destroyed our house as we grew up. We'd get bored in the middle of winter, so we invented the sock fighting game. We took socks, put hard objects in them, and swung them at one another. Our parents warned us, "Don't do this!" While this was an opportunity for us to use wisdom and seek to understand our parents, instead we chose to follow our own opinions. I ended up spending a small fortune paying for new lamps, windows, and other household items.

Ever met people who are hoping to show off their opinions? Many times it's done in a harsh way. Plus, our culture says it's unhealthy to keep our emotions bottled up, so we should just "get it all out." The result? We live in a culture where everyone has an opinion, and there is little to zero listening happening. Francis Martin calls this being "Hung by the Tongue." In other words, the fool will always share what's on his mind, but the wise will think first.

James, the brother of Jesus, has this to say about listening:

James 1:19-20 – *Know this, my beloved brothers: let every person be quick to hear, slow to speak, slow to anger; for the anger of man does not produce the righteousness of God.*

Those of us who are less forthright might be tempted to think that we don't have a problem with being "hung by the tongue." After all, we're not getting into word wars on social media. However, those of us who are less confrontational would do well to remember that gossip is another form of being "hung by the tongue," and its effects at times can be even more damaging.

Ultimately, if our pride and opinions prevent us from seeking understanding and really listening, it can cost us something priceless—the wonder of hearing our Creator communicate to us! God is continually speaking to us. In fact, God is revealing Himself all of the time. There are several ways He does this: He speaks through His Creation (Psalm 19:1-6), through His Word (Psalm 19:7-11), and through the leading of the Spirit (John 14:26).

At a fundamental level, if we want to protect our relationships, see our marriages restored, and thrive in our spiritual journeys, we must, "Seek first to understand, then to be understood." It reminds me of the inscription I saw on a gray slate tombstone at a country church in England: "Beneath this stone, a lump of clay, lies Arabelle Young, who on the 24th of May began to hold her tongue." I wonder how long God was trying to teach her something? How many people did she hurt?

Is there a relationship in your life where you need to first seek to understand before being understood? When was the last time you really just listened without getting distracted by how you would respond? I'm convinced much healing happens when someone is given a safe place to talk. Maybe there's something someone needs to process; maybe there's a story that needs to be shared. Let's choose understanding today!

A Next Step:

Whether you are single or in a relationship, others can most likely identify the words we use that hurt others in our lives. Here's a challenge for today: ask someone you trust, "If you could eliminate one word/phrase from my vocabulary, what would it be?"

_____

_____

_____

_____

_____

_____

_____

_____

DAY 7
GOD CREATED WOMEN AND SEX

Why Christians Should Talk More about Both

– Meredith D.

So ladies, we've come to the day you've either jumped ahead to peek at, or you've been dreading since you opened the Table of Contents. Today is just a discussion about potentially the most intimate area of human life with someone you've never met…not strange at all.

I've had the unique privilege of talking about sex with all kinds of ladies within the church and outside of it. For some reason, I've always been concerned about married couples having a happy, healthy sex life. As believers often grieve for those who have not found Christ, I feel pained when a woman confides in me that her sex life is non-existent or mediocre.

And so, I've met with many ladies alone or in groups to talk about sex and marriage. It's weird, but I've learned to embrace it. I no longer worry about people pointing and saying, "She's the sex lady." My children will probably need therapy someday, and I'm still not sure if my husband is proud or self-conscious. Still, I've learned to embrace it because it's important, and I believe it's helpful to talk about it.

Honestly, nobody is really talking about it in the church. I mean REALLY talking about IT. Not love languages, communicative intimacy, or the hundreds of other ways we avoid talking about sex. However, we have to talk about it. If we don't tackle this issue, the media certainly will. So let's take the topic back from the enemy and quit making it a dirty little secret or a "chore" between a husband and a wife. God created it for our pleasure, so let's enjoy it, as it was intended! Can I get an "Amen?" Too soon?

I know we don't even know each other, and I'm going to talk about something that may be hard for you to discuss with your own husband. Be glad this is a book. I can't ask you a bunch of personal questions and make adolescent jokes. What I will do is give you some of the knowledge I've received from many of my discussions. You may not like or agree with everything. That's okay. Pray about it. Sometimes when I react most strongly to something, it's because it's convicting me and I hate it! I pray that as you read this that God may point you to some areas of your sex life that can be improved or resolved.

The absence of sex in your marriage is serious business. It could be a red flag. You see, our beloved husbands were wired to desire their wives, and we see this in Scripture:

Song of Solomon 7:10 – *I am my beloved's, and his desire is for me.*

It's not a punch line when we talk about how often men think about sex. There are many studies that project the average man thinks about sex anywhere from twenty to two hundred times a day. We can probably agree that sex is critical to your husband, which means it is important to your marriage.

Quit rolling your eyes! I get it. You've heard a thousand times how important sex is to a healthy marriage. You love your husband dearly and don't understand why sex would express that love any more than the other things you do for him. You're a busy woman and setting aside time to get "between the sheets" seems more like a luxury than a necessity. What's the problem? The problem is that's not how he sees it. You probably even already know that too. So…what is stopping us?

The following are the reasons I hear most often. "I'm tired." "The kids need me (or are in the next room)." "My job is super demanding." "I don't feel sexy." "He didn't help me with the household chores, so now I don't have time." "It hurts." "He doesn't know everything about my past." Each one of these reasons is legit. Some are very serious and can definitely impact your sex life. However, if something is causing you to not have sex frequently and happily with your spouse, it's time to talk about it in real terms. Can it be embarrassing or awkward to discuss? Sure! But we've got to get over it. What are the obstacles keeping you from having sex, and what can you can do as a couple to alleviate those roadblocks? Sex is an important component of your marriage; you owe it to each other to give it proper attention. If you don't, it could manifest itself into other parts of your marriage. Don't let the bitterness, resentment, and mind-games spiral downward and out of control. Talk about it and get solutions! Can you let some things go, so you're not tired? Instead of saying "no," say "when" and make sure you keep that commitment. Discuss things he can do to help. Turn your phones and computers off early. Maybe it's time to seek a medical doctor or counselor for help. Whatever the issue is…attack it! Don't sweep it under the rug because you don't think it's that important. It is.

If your level of frequency is not where you both think it should be, then do something about it. Don't believe that it's "just a season" of your life. Seasons have a funny way of turning into the norm. You will always have kids, a sick parent, or a busy job, and the list goes on and on. Make it a priority and not something that's way down on your "to do" list.

Day 7 Key Concept: God created sex, so make it a priority

Unlike what many women think, sex is not just a box to be checked for our guys. A study showed that 65% of the men surveyed listed their number one sex need as mutual satisfaction. That's right; he wants you to enjoy it too! He doesn't want you to be indifferent or begrudgingly agree. Sex is a way he shows you he loves you and wants to connect with you. As women, we tend to want to connect with our spouses and then have sex. For most guys, that connection and closeness comes after we have sex with them. It's also important to him as a man that you believe he is good at sex. Gently talk about what is not doing it for you and be encouraging when something is amazing. He's not a mind reader. Once a lady told me that she and her hubby of fifteen years never talked about sex. When asked why, she said, "It's embarrassing." I challenged her to go home and have an honest talk with him about their sex life. When I followed up with her, she said it started off really awkward but continued by saying they had the best sex the rest of the week. Worth it!

When is the last time you initiated sex? Is he always the one to approach you? So many times we forget to initiate with our husbands. Be sexy, be silly, be creative, be impulsive. I had a wife once tell me that she "isn't that creative in the bedroom." I don't buy it! You are brilliant in many areas of your life. You have MacGyvered things like school projects, family dinners, and office presentations into works of art with limited time and resources. Give this area of your marriage the same thoughtful attention. Who cares if it's an epic fail. Laugh about it! You at least put yourself out there and that should get great levels of appreciation from your hubby. I'm sure he would also be willing to share some of his fantasies or desires.

As a side note, if you're always the one making the effort, you may want to think about the following: Is your husband ill? Perhaps there's an underlying sickness that is causing him to not feel up to it. Is there an addiction to pornography or an extra-marital affair? Is there some unresolved anger in your marriage? Or (don't hurt me) are you a controlling wife? This can be a hard pill to swallow. If your husband doesn't think he can please you anywhere else, why would he make himself so vulnerable in the bedroom? I've had ladies get angry with me for mentioning this to them, but they've later come back and said they've become a "nagging" wife without realizing it. I'm not saying your man is King David, Solomon, and Jesus wrapped up in one husband. I'm not saying that he is perfect and never does anything wrong. But maybe take a closer look at how you speak to him. Are you starting to sound more like his mom than his lover?

Lastly, are you praying about your sex life? It might feel a little odd, but remember we are to take everything to God in prayer. Why wouldn't we take this important and crucial part of our marriage to Him, as well? Don't be ashamed or afraid to bring issues before our wonderful, loving God. Pray that your husband desires your touch and you his touch.

Song of Solomon 5:16 – *His mouth is most sweet, and he is altogether most desirable. This is my beloved and this is my friend, O daughters of Jerusalem.*

Now, let's apply truth! And if you're a husband, please don't highlight certain sentences for your wife. Pray the Holy Spirit speaks to both of you.

A Next Step:

How women see themselves and their spouses is critical to a healthy sexual dynamic in marriage. Your husband needs to know that you are thinking about him. Today, plan some time just to be with him…a date night without the kids, a night out of town, or a weekend getaway.

_____

_____

_____

_____

_____

_____

_____

_____

_____

_____

_____

_____

_____

_____

_____

_____

_____

_____

_____

_____

_____

_____

_____

_____

_____

_____

_____

_____

_____

_____

_____

_____

_____

_____

_____

_____

_____

_____

_____

DAY 8

JUST CALL ON ME, BROTHER

Navigating the Single Life

– Gail H.

I spent the better part of my 20s and 30s looking for a relationship, wishing I was in a relationship, wondering why I wasn't in a relationship…you get the picture. I would tell myself that maybe some guy would like me if I lost a little weight or wore prettier clothes. When I looked around, all of my friends were meeting people, getting married, and having kids; it seemed so easy for them. As each friend settled into family life and no longer had as much time to hang out with friends, the lonelier I felt.

Loneliness is something everyone deals with from time to time, but for a single person it's very easy to become isolated. In fact, it can happen quickly.

It can mean going months without something as simple as a hug from anyone or starting a weekend knowing that nobody would even know if something happened to you, until you don't show up for work on Monday. These thoughts and circumstances can (and did for me) lead to issues with anxiety and depression.

If you do a Google search, you can find dozens of articles and statistics about the growing numbers of older singles, both in America and in American churches. While the numbers are increasing across the board, singleness in the church is still generally viewed as being "pre-married." There can sometimes be an almost tangible chasm between couples and singles in the church. For example, there are couples and family small groups, and there are singles small groups. I've been in both at one time or another. As a single in a couple's group, the people in my group were awesome, but there was little socializing outside of the time we met each week. Everyone had a significant other, and as more kids came along, less time was available to be active in each other's lives. In the singles groups, there was definitely more time for being social, but I still felt out of place. The majority of people were just a few years out of college, while I was up to ten years older than most of them.

How do we, as singles, navigate a world geared towards couples and families? How do we navigate a world where well-meaning married friends have no concept of how it feels to come home each night to an empty house where nobody wonders how your day was? How do we embrace being single, even if we wish we weren't? How do we get past the loneliness?

Day 8 Key Concept: Everybody needs somebody

I'd been struggling to write about the incredibly broad topic of singleness. I knew I didn't want to focus on how to deal with the negatives of not being in a romantic relationship, but I did want to discuss how crucial it is to have single friends and/or married friends who include you in their lives. I'd been praying about it, and then inspiration came along in a very unexpected way. I recently went to a concert and heard a song I'd heard dozens of times before—"Lean on Me" by Bill Withers. This song is so well known, but hearing it this time, the familiar lyrics hit me in a new way:

> *You just call on me brother when you need a hand.*
> *We all need somebody to lean on.*
> *I just might have a problem that you'll understand.*
> *We all need somebody to lean on.*

These lyrics helped me understand a solution to the problem of loneliness. The songwriter doesn't say that some people need someone to lean on or even that most people need somebody. He says we ALL need someone. The heart of the song is to be a friend and know you need a friend, as well.

Interestingly, there is biblical truth in this classic song. Throughout Scripture, we find many verses on the importance of having a brother, a neighbor, a friend. We all do need someone to lean on.

Ecclesiastes 4:9-10 – *Two are better than one, because they have a good reward for their toil. For if they fall, one will lift up his fellow. But woe to him who is alone when he falls and has not another to life him up!*

Proverbs 27:10 – *Better is a neighbor who is near than a brother who is far away.*

Galatians 6:2 – *Bear one another's burdens, and so fulfill the law of Christ.*

For single people, it is imperative to have close friends. Everyone needs people with whom to do life. I spent ten years living alone in a cute little house wishing I wasn't alone, but I'd unintentionally isolated myself with expert precision. After ten years, God provided for me in ways I didn't even know I desperately needed. A good friend of mine saw what I was going through and suggested I start seeing a counselor. Through that process, God put another single girl close to my own age in my life. Through friendship (we've been close friends for just over five years now, and it's been an amazing gift!) and counseling, I've been able to see how I was the main cause of my loneliness.

You might be thinking, "That's great that God dropped a friend right into your life, but what about me? He hasn't done that for me!" The answer to that question is threefold.

- Pray for single friends
- Seek out single friends
- Be the friend that you are seeking

It's not easy to find good friends once you get in to your 30s, and unfortunately it's easy to have a pity party about how all of your friends are married and you're just stuck alone. So, ask people you know, ask your pastor, and ask people at other churches. The statistics tell us there are a lot of single people in the church today, so we need to find and befriend each other. I honestly didn't realize how isolated I was, until I wasn't anymore.

To the married folks and couples who aren't sure how to relate to the singles around them: look for us, notice us, introduce us to each other, and don't be afraid to invite us into your lives. Many of us don't mind being the third, fifth, or seventh wheel at all.

I imagine that many single people will grab this book on relationships, check out the Table of Contents, and wonder how many chapters or parts of chapters can help those who are single. I see things that way a lot of times. I want to encourage you that relationship skills, especially communication skills, definitely affect friendships as well as marriages. I pray that God helps all of us find someone to lean on.

A Next Step:

If you are currently single, think about how you can spend more intentional time with friends. Maybe you need to add some friends to your life. If you are married, your natural tendency is going to be spending time with other married folks. Think about how you can intentionally broaden your family circle to include folks who are not married.

_____
_____
_____
_____
_____
_____
_____
_____
_____
_____
_____
_____
_____
_____
_____
_____
_____
_____
_____

DAY 9

WHEN TYPE A MARRIES TYPE B

How to Preach the Gospel into Your Marriage

– Allison M.

About five months after my husband and I were married, we were off to spend our first Thanksgiving with my side of the family. I told my mom we'd be heading up to Cleveland at around 10 a.m., so when Thanksgiving morning arrived, I woke up early, got ready, and noticed that while the morning was quickly passing, my husband was not quickly getting ready. No sweat, I thought. He's probably just planning on taking a quick shower. He knows what time we're supposed to be leaving. Well, the next thing I know, it was a little past 10 a.m., my husband was still in the shower, and I'm pretty sure my head was about to explode.

You see, in my family, if you say you're leaving at 10 a.m., what that actually means is that at 9:59 a.m., you're in the car and buckling your seatbelts (safety first!). At precisely 10 a.m., you are pulling out of the driveway with a full tank of gas that you bought the day before to ensure nothing would slow you down. However, in my husband's family, if you say you're leaving at 10 a.m., what that really means is you're planning on leaving around 10 a.m. What that looks like is that at 10:05 a.m. you're pulling your clothes out of the dryer, and when you hop into the car, you decide you need to stop by Starbucks to grab a coffee and fill up the old gas tank because you've been on empty since yesterday.

When I first met my husband, his way of life was one of the things I loved most about him—he was relaxed, easy going, and spontaneous (everything I was not). However, after we were married and doing life together, suddenly those beloved differences that you think are so cute can become areas of stress. See I loved him for who he was, but I expected him to NOT be that way in certain situations (i.e. whenever I wanted him to operate how I do. That seems fair, right?).

That first Thanksgiving morning was a bit of a wake-up call for me. I felt a nudge from God deep down in my heart reminding me of the core of Christianity—that we are ALL sinners in need of a Savior.

Romans 3:23-24 – *for all have sinned and fall short of the glory of God, and are justified by his grace as a gift, through the redemption that is in Christ Jesus*

To be honest, on that morning I thought I was right and my husband was wrong. He should do things my family's way, not his family's way. However, the truth of God's word helped me remember that I don't get everything right. I'm just a flawed, messed-up, broken person in need of God's saving grace. Even though I like to think I'm right most (or all) of the time, I'm not.

The Gospel message, the idea that we are all terribly flawed, sinful, and in need of God's grace to us through His Son Jesus, has been the great helper to me in my marriage, especially when things aren't going exactly as I expect they should. The Gospel helps me remember that I, too, am a mess, even though it's perhaps easier to forget and hide from others because I get my "to-do" lists done or show up on time. But in the end, we all need the forgiveness of God because of our sinful hearts.

Day 9 Key Concept: The Gospel is the great equalizer

My husband operates very differently than me. It's God's grace to us through Jesus that helps me see and remember that I'm not right, and he's not wrong— we're just different. And, by the way, I'm thankful for those differences. He helps me to slow down, laugh more, enjoy life more, and go get a Krispy Kreme donut when the hot sign is on, which is something I probably wouldn't have done without him (it would have been a little too spontaneous for super-planned me). He's also been helped by our differences—he now creates a weekly to do list for our home and helps me get all of our kids ready in the morning, so we can be out the door in good time.

I can honestly say that I would be an absolutely terrible wife without Jesus. I think my ego, my pride, and my Type A personality would have me thinking that my spouse was always at fault, whenever I encountered a problem in my marriage. I imagine thoughts such as, "If he would just…" would be running constantly through my mind, inflating my ego while letting all of the air out of my relationship. But praise God, as He reminds us that none of us are better than the other, none of us are without sin, and all of us are flawed beyond what we could even imagine.

No wonder God desires us to read and know His word. Throughout Scripture, we are constantly reminded of man's sinful heart. Even the people we think are really godly still have big time sin issues. Think about King David's affair or the Apostle Peter's three denials. I love that God's word tells us these stories because we need to see again and again and again what people really are—a mess. Jesus even reminds us of this in Luke 18:19 when he tells the rich ruler, "No one is good except God alone." How much more beautiful is God's love for us when we realize how spiritually bankrupt we really are? The fact that He knows everything about us, sees everything we do, and still loves us is just amazing.

Preach the gospel to yourself constantly. Remind yourself of who you actually are. You're not perfect. You do things wrong. You make mistakes of all kinds, big and small, and you have a wicked, wicked heart.

Then, remember God's unconditional love for you and extend that love to your spouse. Don't expect them to be perfect; they are not and neither are you. See yourself and your spouse the way God does; it enables you to admit you're wrong, say, "I'm sorry," and love each other well.

A Next Step:

Someone once said, "Expectations are everything in marriage." Ask your spouse today, "What is one expectation that you had coming into our relationship that has changed?" Then, take the opportunity to share one as well. If you are single, how have your expectations about relationships both blessed and created conflict in your relationships?

_____

_____

_____

_____

_____

_____

_____

_____

_____

_____

_____

DAY 10

MARRIAGE AND MONEY

How to Keep Finances from Causing Fights

– Brad C.

Can you bring to mind the dumbest fight you've ever had in your marriage? Hopefully, it brings a smile to your face as you think back to how silly and insignificant it was. For my wife and me, it was whether or not it was appropriate to wear pajamas to the midnight buffet on our honeymoon cruise. For what it's worth, I still think I'm right!

Thankfully, in just a little over twenty years of marriage, habitual conflict has not been a dominant theme. Still, anytime you put two sinful people into a long-term relationship, a life completely devoid of conflict is simply unrealistic. Because of our sin nature, we naturally gravitate towards pursuing our own self-interests. In other words, I am a big fan of me.

For the past seventeen years, I've been called upon dozens of times to facilitate pre-marital counseling for young couples, and I always include a session on conflict and the biblical principles for resolving it in a Christ-honoring way. I also point out the common landmines in marriage—money, sex, parenting, and expectations. Others in this book will offer great wisdom on the last three, but my hope is to provide some biblical help with the first. And according to research, we need both help and hope as it relates to navigating finances in the context of marriage.

Consider the following:

- 56% of all divorces cite financial stress as one of the leading factors in pursuing divorce according to one study.
- In another study, financial stress was listed as the second leading cause of divorce, right behind infidelity.

National statistics about personal finance are discouraging to say the least, and often individuals only compound their financial woes upon marrying.

But the good news is that God's word is not silent on the subject. Nearly half of all the Bible's parables deal with money and possessions, and there are over 2,350 verses about them as well. So we can find help and hope for life in the Scriptures in very practical areas, including how to handle money. We'd be wise to avoid "leaning unto our own understanding"

(Proverbs 3). Instead, we should follow God's wisdom for handling our finances.

Day 10 Key Concept: Understand the currency of God's economy

The following guidelines have been helpful in my own marriage. And they've served as guardrails for other marriages that I've attempted to help make cents (see what I did there!) of the mystery of personal finances.

Principle #1: Understand the biblical purpose of money

Maybe you've heard this claim before—money changes people. While that idea is often repeated, I wouldn't agree. In fact, I would argue that money does NOT change people, but rather it magnifies who they already are. Give a generous person a million dollars, and he or she will find ways to give it away. Give greedy people a quarter, and they'll take it to their grave. The reason is because we become like what we worship. If I worship money, I can't bear the thought of giving any away because, in doing so, I forfeit some of my identity. And when someone challenges our identity—especially in marriage—that's a recipe for conflict.

So, what is the biblical purpose for money? It's simple—worship. Money should be used as a vehicle for worship. Proverbs 3:9 says, "Honor the Lord with your wealth." Giving honor to the Lord is an act of worship. From the very beginning of humanity, God asked people to give offerings, not because He needed something from us, but because He desired to be the object of our worship and giving is an overflow of our worship.

If the Bible teaches that worship is a lifestyle, which it does, then there are very few areas of life where I have greater opportunity to worship God than with my wealth. While not everyone gets married and not everyone has children, almost everyone will have an opportunity to handle money. The question is whether or not we'll view it as God does: as an act of worship. This is important because the ultimate goal of handling money in marriage shouldn't be to gain the approval or avoid the scorn of our spouse—it should be to please Christ.

Principle #2: Understand what it means to be a steward

Here is one of my favorite stewardship passages in the Bible:

1 Chronicles 29:11-12 – *Yours, O Lord, is the greatness, the power, the glory, the victory, and the majesty. Everything in the heavens and on earth is yours, O Lord, and this is your kingdom. We adore you as the one who is over all things. Wealth and honor come from you alone, for you rule over everything. Power and might are in your hand, and at your discretion people are made great and given strength. (NLT)*

This passage teaches us two clear principles: everything comes FROM God and everything belongs TO God. Settling the issue of ownership is the most important decision you will ever make related to money and finances. Remember, God isn't looking for you to just be a good money manager; He is looking for hearts that are surrendered to Him. The purpose of the Gospel is not to just change our behavior ("Look how well I can handle money!"). It's to reorient the affections of our heart ("I trust God with all that I've been given"). So, the Gospel transforms the inner man, not merely creating a more financially savvy outer man.

So, what practical difference does this make in marriage? You and your spouse should have the same foundation when it comes to how you handle money. The result? You both approach your finances with the deep conviction that God is the owner, and you are simply the manager or steward. And what does a manager do? Whatever the owner asks Him to do.

If a husband and wife approach money with this base conviction, it does two things. First, it releases them from trying to get their way, as if they were owners as opposed to managers. Second, it takes the pressure and stress off of financial decisions. You don't have to rely upon your spouse to come up with great financial strategies to provide stability to your marriage. You simply have to follow the Owner's instructions.

Principle #3: Guard your marriage against deceptive communication

Consider the following statistic: One-third of people who admitted to arguing with their spouse about money say they hid a purchase because their spouse wouldn't approve. Now, contrast that with the biblical picture of communication in Ephesians 4 where the Apostle Paul writes, "speak the truth in love" (verse 15) and "stop telling lies"(verse 25). Those verses don't take a theological education to understand. But despite the clarity of those truths, communication regarding money is a common source of deceptive communication.

One of the practices I consistently counsel couples away from is setting up separate checking accounts. Separate checking accounts provide practical means to be deceptive regarding money in marriage. I'm not alone in this counsel. Personal finance guru Dave Ramsey offers the following advice: "I haven't marked it down nor actually kept up with it in research, but over the twenty years of financial counseling, when I have a spouse who is demanding separate accounts, a disturbing number of times I discover an affair, because they're planning to leave. They're wanting a separate life because they have a secret life."[1]

In addition, Art Rainer, author of *The Marriage Challenge*, shares the following wise counsel: "One of the very first pieces of advice I gave was to, once married, get joint bank accounts and avoid bank accounts to which your spouse will not be able to access. Why? Because you do not get choose what part of your spouse you want to marry or what part you want to give to your spouse. It's an all-in deal—You get all of them, and they get all of you."[2]

He lists five reasons why he counsels against the practice of having separate checking accounts.

- A joint account communicates "our money."
- A joint account communicates "our expenditures."
- A joint account communicates transparency.
- A joint account communicates trust.
- A joint account communicates commitment.[3]

Marriage is hard! Don't make it harder by neglecting the Master's counsel on managing money. The old saying really is true—Father knows best.

A Next Step:

In most relationships, one person is the spender and the other person is more of a saver. Where do you fall on that spectrum? If you don't have a budget, take the opportunity to download a free budget worksheet at financialpeaceuniversity.com.

_____

_____

_____

_____

_____

_____

DAY 11
WORKING THROUGH A MARRIAGE CRISIS

Finding the Upside of Down

– Derek & Rachel H.

"Create in me a pure heart, O God, and renew a steadfast spirit within me. Do not cast me from your presence or take your Holy Spirit from me. Restore to me the joy of your salvation and grant me a willing spirit, to sustain me. Then I will teach transgressors your ways, and sinners will turn back to you." Psalm 51:10-13 (NIV)

When disaster strikes, where do you turn? Where do you go when your life seems to be falling apart?

Who do you run to when YOU'RE the reason your world is broken?

I'd just accepted a promotion at work, and the new job involved taking my family and moving to Florida. I was stoked, and my wife, Rachel, was extremely supportive of me and the upcoming transition for our family. At that time, both Rachel and I would have described our marriage as strong and healthy. We had two young boys and were looking forward to a new adventure together.

Once we arrived in our new city and started to settle in, my new job proved to be very demanding and had me traveling often. At first, I really enjoyed climbing the corporate ladder and was excited about the early success and momentum. I didn't realize it at that time, but in hindsight, I know that I'd shifted much of my time and attention away from God and poured most of it into work. While we still attended church every week and even a small group, I wasn't in God's Word on a daily basis and didn't have any accountability from other Christian brothers because I wasn't seeking out those relationships. As a result, I developed a newfound sense of pride, as my burgeoning success tricked me into believing I could handle anything. I was about to find out how perilous that mindset would prove to be.

A number of months passed, and I found myself in one of the worst possible situations imaginable. I was traveling for work and hanging out with colleagues over dinner and drinks. I typically didn't have more than one or two drinks, but that night I regretfully had way too much. The next day I woke up in a daze and came to the shocking realization that I'd been unfaithful to my wife. I was devastated and overwhelmed with sorrow. I immediately wondered how could this happen and how my wife could ever forgive me? Would I lose my family forever? How could a Christian do such a thing? I was utterly broken and spent the next week in complete despair. Shortly thereafter, I was able to get with a Christian counselor who helped and encouraged me to turn back to God and ask for forgiveness. The next step would be telling my wife what had happened and asking for her forgiveness.

During this internal struggle with how and when to tell my wife, I knew God was working in my heart. While I felt His amazing forgiveness, at the same time, there was a burden that wouldn't be lifted until I confessed my sin to my wife. I knew that I had to trust in the Lord and be honest, even if it meant potentially losing my family. A decent amount of time had passed since my catastrophic sin, and I knew I couldn't wait any longer. This unconfessed sin was holding me back in my relationship with the Lord. I shared what had happened with a couple of close friends, and we began to pray for that upcoming conversation with Rachel. I was unaware that God was already speaking to her and preparing her heart to walk through this season of grief. In His kindness, God enabled Rachel to trust that whatever was coming, He was going to bring her through it. I finally confessed to her what I'd done. It was heartbreaking to watch her walk through it and try to comprehend how this could've happened. Even though I knew that God had already forgiven me, it felt very much that now God was able to break up the fallow ground of my heart (Hosea 10:12).

As Rachel experienced the emotional highs and lows, I discovered it was important to simply be there to listen and answer questions. This wasn't the time to sink back into my old prideful thinking and focus on myself. In fact, this was the time for me to just trust God, as simple as that might sound. I needed God to truly meet both of our needs, and I trusted that He would sustain my marriage, children, relationships... everything. It was only when I acquired that attitude, recognizing how incapable I was of holding my life together, that God allowed me to be the humble, gentle, and supportive husband that Rachel needed through this. I needed to be open with her and help her work through the deep hurt I'd caused. When she didn't feel comfortable with me traveling or found certain triggers that caused her additional anguish, I had to be willing to honor her above myself (Romans 12:10). While I recognized how difficult this time was for her, it was a struggle for me too. Each time Rachel went through a season of struggle, feelings of guilt and despair would creep into my mind. I realized that I needed the Holy Spirit to give me the patience required, no matter how long the healing process would take. Even more, I needed to die to my old self and let Christ do His work in me and restore our marriage.

Through this crisis, Rachel was a true model of Christ's love and forgiveness, which was propelled by her spending time in God's Word. She was the one who forgave me and wanted nothing more than to work through this. Even though she was hurting profoundly at times, she showed me grace, compassion, and unconditional love that I've never felt from another person in my life. We both give God the glory for the work He did in Rachel's heart, by showing her that I couldn't fulfill all of her needs—only God could do that. He was working in my heart as well by changing me and showing me a kind of mercy I'd never experienced before. It was a terrifying step, confessing my sin, because it meant I could lose my family; however, God was gracious and gave me a deep sense of acceptance that I so desperately needed after such a huge moral failure.

In Scripture, we read about so many who have experienced pain and sorrow, and yet we also see the goodness of God who shows up in the midst of their agony. In the Book of Job, after God had brought Job through a tremendous time of loss, Job says, "My ears have heard of You, but now my eyes have seen You" (Job 42:5). Job's suffering allowed him to experience God more. The same is true for us—when we walk through dark times, we get a clearer picture of God's sovereignty, wisdom, and kindness.

Day 11 Key Concept: God redeems the dark days

After a couple of years, Rachel and I both felt that God had not only wholly restored our marriage, but He also made it stronger in an entirely new way. There was a newfound trust and better communication. In addition, God gave us the opportunity to more fully seek Him together as a couple, as we've both refocused on having daily quiet time in Scripture and a prayer time together. After my confession to Rachel, she noticed I was growing considerably in my personal relationship with the Lord, which God used to affirm to her that He is faithful as we genuinely seek Him.

Fast-forward to today, and God has blessed us mightily in so many ways: our marriage, our children, and also the ministry areas that He's opened up for us. God allows us to see His activity as we are walking with Him, and His grace has spurred us to have a deep desire to serve where we are called. This includes serving in multiple areas—together. God continues to open doors for us to counsel and love others who are going through their own struggles in marriage. Why can we do this? Because He is able to do immeasurably more than all we ask or imagine, according to His power that is at work within us (Ephesians 3:20). In addition, instead of being so focused on climbing the corporate ladder, God has opened the door to counsel others in the business community. Before this all happened, I wasn't focused on being a light to others in the business world, but now God has given me that chance because He works all things for the good of those who love Him (Romans 8:28).

In the end, Rachel and I are seeking the Lord together, and as we walk through life's highs and lows, our prayer is that God would continually draw us to Himself.

A Next Step:

If you are facing a crisis, don't do it alone. Find someone you trust with a godly perspective to give you wisdom. Too many times, we tend to listen to the wrong people in moments of crisis. Remember that you most likely did not arrive here in one day, so this crisis most likely won't be solved in one day.

_____
_____
_____
_____
_____
_____
_____
_____
_____
_____
_____
_____
_____
_____
_____
_____
_____

DAY 12
BASIC TRAINING

Why Discipleship is Man's Best Friend
– Brendan & Kristi N.

"Love the LORD your God with all your heart and with all your soul and with all your strength. These commandments that I give you today are to be on your hearts. Impress them on your children. Talk about them when you sit at home and when you walk along the road, when you lie down, and when you get up. Tie them as symbols on your hands and bind them on your foreheads. Write them on the doorframes of your houses and on your gates." Deuteronomy 6:5-9 (NIV)

Picture the cutest yellow Labrador puppy you can possibly imagine. Soft, floppy ears. Oversized paws.

And, of course, those puppy dog eyes that could turn Scrooge into Cupid. For our family, that puppy has a name—Simone—and she was with us for fifteen months. She has been loved on, played with, and faithfully trained by everyone in our family. And what was once the cutest puppy ever has now grown into what we believe might be the best dog ever!

Now, imagine the conflicting emotions that would come with turning Simone back to her rightful owner to complete her training and fulfill her purpose on this earth. Recently, we experienced the mixed emotions of heartbreak, sadness, joy, and anticipation in doing just that...Simone was not ours to keep, because she is a Canine Companion puppy. We volunteered (initially against my better judgment) to be puppy raisers with the complete knowledge and understanding that the day would come when it would be time to return Simone. Canine Companions for Independence is a non-profit organization that enhances the lives of people with disabilities by providing highly trained assistance dogs. These incredible dogs open new opportunities and possibilities, while spreading endless joy to their owners.

Simone was bred specifically to be the perfect companion for someone desperately needing her help. From the moment she was born, Simone had a purpose and we were blessed enough to be selected as her puppy raisers to help her fulfill that purpose.

You may be thinking, "Why in the world would anyone sign up for that?" Volunteering for emotional heartbreak along with long-term psychological counseling for the whole family...sounds horrible, doesn't it? Or does it? Or does it remind you of something called "parenting?"

As parents, we are given a finite amount of time to raise our children—18 years, 216 months, or 6,570 days. In that time, we must introduce them to faith in Jesus Christ, educate them to the truths of the Bible, train them to use their faith to live a life of obedience, and foster in them a boldness and desire to witness to the saving grace of the Gospel. This is a tall order for sure! However, it is our highest calling as parents...not to be taken lightly or left to chance. Such a mission must be intentional, if it is to be successful.

Key 12 Concept: Discipling your children must be intentional, if it's going to be successful

Here's a definition:

> A **Christian Disciple** is one who accepts to the core the saving grace of the Gospel, the truths of the Bible, and faithfully assists in spreading the good news of these beliefs.

> **Discipling another** would be the act of purposefully and intentionally using your faith in Jesus Christ to point others to Him by actively demonstrating a life committed to these principles and training others to apply the truth of Scripture.

Here are some things we have learned in trying to apply this to our family:

1. According to Scripture, the first step is to be resolute in your own faith and consistent in your own spiritual discipline.

Deuteronomy 6:5-6 – *Love the LORD your God with all your heart and with all your soul and with all your strength. These commandments that I give you today are to be on your hearts.*

It is unrealistic to believe that you can successfully train up a disciple, if you are not obedient and committed to be the same.

2. The second step is to talk about your faith and the passion of your convictions with your children consistently.

Deuteronomy 6:7-8 – *Impress them on your children. Talk about them when you sit at home and when you walk along the road, when you lie down, and when you get up. Tie them as symbols on your hands bind them on your foreheads.*

Your children watch you and see what you do and how you respond in situations, BUT they will never know why you do what you do or respond the way you do without you sharing with them. This is where concepts like honesty and transparency mingle with repentance, grace, and forgiveness. Don't worry! YOU DON'T HAVE TO BE PERFECT. Jesus was perfect in our place. You just have to be perfectly humble and honest.

3. The third principle we have learned is to out-
    wardly profess your beliefs and use everyday
    situations to apply your faith.

Deuteronomy 6:9 – *Write them on the doorframes*
of your houses and on your gates.

> While being a disciple isn't easy, it also doesn't have
> to be complicated. Take a deep breath; you don't have
> to come up with a detailed lesson plan or in-depth
> curriculum. You have been given all the teaching aids
> needed in the truth of the Bible and the example of
> Jesus. Use these as your guides and allow the realities
> of everyday life to be your classroom. Be creative!

As we asked earlier about our adorable little
puppy, Simone: "Why would anyone sign up for
such a bag of mixed emotions?"

At the time of this writing, our family consists of
my wife and me, six children (ranging in age from
11 to 29), a daughter-in-law, two grandsons, and
two future sons-in-law. I am only certain of one
thing: our family dynamic will be ever changing.
And the rhythms of our family life will differ with
every change. That is a good thing because our
opportunities to experience God, to grow spiritually,
and to disciple and be discipled will also differ with
each unique change.

When we started praying and searching for a
unique opportunity to provide discipleship opportunities for our family and practice our witness in
the community around us, the Lord gave us Simone.
So when we agreed to be puppy raisers, our family

purposefully and intentionally entered into the time with a definitive understanding that Simone would be part of a mission for our family. As we prayed, here's what we sensed:

- Caring for Simone would allow our whole family to participate and foster family bonds and teaching points.
- This would open opportunities for meaningful conversations and possible church/faith invitations to people we encountered. (Nothing creates a draw like an adorable puppy wearing a service cape!)
- Our children would learn the disciplines of training, consistency, and persistence.
- Our family would learn how our sacrifice could bless others.

God accomplished all of this through a dog!

In the end, we helped Simone fulfill her purpose, and we pray that she will be a light to the world and a blessing to all she encounters. Isn't that the point of discipleship? As parents, if you disciple your children well, a time will come when you launch them into the world. The countdown is on. Make today count!

A Next Step:

Where are spaces in your life that you can create
intentional moments for spiritual conversations?
You can not only bless your children, but you can
bless other children, as well. You don't have to be
a parent to encourage a young person. As a matter
of fact, kids may tend to listen to others MORE
than their parents at times. Today, pray and ask
God where those moments are and who those
people are for you connect with.

_____

_____

_____

_____

_____

_____

_____

_____

_____

_____

_____

_____

_____

_____

_____

_____

_____

_____

_____

_____

_____

_____

_____

_____

_____

_____

_____

_____

_____

_____

_____

_____

_____

_____

_____

_____

_____

_____

_____

_____

_____

_____

DAY 13
RELATIONSHIPS, ANXIETY, & DEPRESSION

Finding Light in the Darkness
— Ryan B.

This was the moment I'd looked forward to for almost a year. I had returned home from a combat tour in Iraq and my wife, Amber, and I were on a date night at my favorite Japanese steak house. We weren't able to communicate much during that year, so we had a lot of catching up to do. In fact, I was so dialed into our conversation that I didn't realize the chef had arrived at our table and begun his routine. If you've ever been to a Japanese steak house, you know that the chef typically puts on quite a show before starting to cook. Out of nowhere, and to my great surprise, the chef lit a fire on the grill that shot straight up in the air. At the same time, I shot directly back in my chair and fell to the ground. Everyone in the restaurant erupted with laughter, as did Amber and I. But deep down, I was terrified. Little did I know, that night would provide the first glimpse into a lifelong struggle with anxiety and depression.

Regardless of the cause of your anxiety and depression, the common effect on you personally and your marriage can be tragic. I may not understand what you are dealing with on a personal level, but I do know that many others, including myself, have walked the same path in having such a struggle. I also find it extremely comforting that the Bible is not silent when it comes to walking through dark times.

Listen to how David describes his feelings openly and honestly, as he prays:

Psalm 13:1 – *How long, O* Lord? Will you for-get me forever? *How long will you hide your face from me?*

David was no stranger to dealing with the emotional stressors of life. Some were caused by his own sin, while others were caused by outside forces beyond his control. Either way, his emotions and heartfelt pleas to Jehovah-God resonate with all of us. What David wrestled with during his darkest moments is comparable to what many Christians wrestle with today. Specifically, how do I reconcile my anxious, depressive emotions against the back-drop of my faith in a good and loving God? Maybe you have asked questions or made statements like these before:

- Why do I feel so depressed (or anxious or angry), when I have a pretty good life?
- Do I feel this way because I don't have enough faith?
- If I just try harder, then these problems will go away eventually.
- Maybe I am not a real Christian if I do not have joy or feel so anxious.

Day 13 Key Concept: Fight back the darkness by running to the light

Here are three things Amber and I have learned during my journey of fighting this battle.

1. Fight the urge to ignore.

At first, my problems didn't seem like a big deal. For example, I'd be in a crowded room, and all of a sudden, I'd begin to feel very nervous and uncomfortable. I'd think maybe the room was just too hot, so I tried wearing lighter clothing. Still, that didn't seem to make any difference. Also, sleep began to be an issue. Sometimes I'd have trouble sleeping or even falling asleep. Other nights, I'd wake up in the middle of the night and not be able to fall back asleep. I tried taking sleep medication, but even that didn't seem to help. As a result, I became very irritable and the smallest things seemed to set me off in anger. A minor disagreement with Amber would turn into a big argument, and when it was over, I had no idea how things had escalated so quickly. I'd try to be more patient with Amber and the kids, but that didn't seem to work either. These were all signs that something more serious was happening inside. My default mode was to ignore the signs and keep moving forward. However, it's important to take inventory of your feelings and emotions on a consistent basis. If you feel as though something is off, address it. There is power in naming your problems and bringing them into the Light.

    2. Fight the urge to isolate.

The American independent mindset can be an amazing thing, when it comes to innovation and the drive to succeed. However, this same mindset can steer you towards disaster when dealing with anxiety and depression. This was the hardest lesson for me to learn. I took a great amount of pride in being a "self-made" man. Unfortunately, my pride caused me to isolate myself from those around me whenever I felt anxious or depressed. A big part of why I chose to ignore my problems was that I thought I could handle them on my own. Much like any other obstacle I'd faced, I wrongly believed that if I put my head down, worked hard, and tried to be a good person, eventually good things would happen and my problems would go away. Still, I rarely felt that I was winning in life, which in turn made me feel more depressed. Eventually, I pulled away from people because I felt shame; I felt as though I failed. Even more, I believed no one could possibly understand what I was going through, so why even bother asking for help? It took many difficult and lonely years to realize that I needed others in my life to walk with me during my toughest seasons. I started by meeting with my pastor. Through his counsel, I slowly started talking to Amber about what I was going through. With Amber's love and encouragement, we started attending a Lifegroup together at our church with other couples where I shared my story and problems. It didn't happen overnight, but over time my life shifted from being very lonely and hopeless to very connected and supported. My encouragement is to start small. Talk to your spouse about what you are feeling or talk with a pastor or a trusted friend. Know that you will want to isolate yourself from others, so take the steps now to connect relationally to people you trust.

3. Fight the urge to self-medicate.

About a month after I returned home from Iraq, I found myself sitting alone on the couch, drinking beer, eating chips, and binge-watching Band of Brothers...and I stayed that way for ten days. Looking back, it's easy to see that I was self-medicating. At the time, however, I called it relaxing. You may call it a different name: unwinding, escaping, or taking the edge off, but the deeper reality remains the same—it is self-medication. There are so many ways that I tried to self-medicate over years; the list would be too long to name. Regardless, anytime I felt anxious or depressed, I reached for something to help dull the pain inside. It was only after years of professional counseling that I realized I was self-medicating to fill a void that only God could fill. Let me be clear. I am NOT saying that a relationship with God will automatically solve your problems or take away your emotional struggles. What I am saying is that ultimately only God will provide the comfort and rest you desire most. At the beginning of Psalm 13, we see that David is a broken man, tormented on the inside, and wrestling with deep spiritual questions, but after he bares his soul to God, he finishes his prayer this way:

Psalm 13:6 – I will sing to the Lord, because he has dealt bountifully with me.

David asked God many hard questions throughout this Psalm, none of which were answered easily or immediately. However, David made a choice. He chose to praise God and trust Him fully based on God's good character. Notice that David didn't chose to praise God because God had solved all of his problems. Rather, it was an active choice to find satisfaction in God rather than something else. You and I face the same choice each day between self-medication and God-medication, if you will.

For spouses who are walking alongside a loved one dealing with anxiety and depression, please know that you, too, are not alone. The steps I outlined for your loved one hold true for you as well. It's not easy being a support system for someone in midst of anxiety and depression, so don't ignore your own feelings as you walk through it. Enlist others to come alongside to support you in the same way you are being supportive to your struggling spouse. Remember that God is faithful and trustworthy. When you do not feel grace towards your spouse, lean on God as the Author of grace to fill your cup as each day passes.

A Next Step:

Depression and anxiety wear many faces in our culture. Sometimes, people will fight those battles for a lifetime. Other times, people will struggle for seasons or just during specific circumstances. Mercy is a fruit of God's Spirit working in our lives. Is there someone that you may need to extend mercy to, who may be walking this journey right now?

_____

_____

_____

_____

_____

_____

_____

_____

_____

DAY 14
HISTORY CLASS

Getting Past Your Past

– Heather T.

Throughout our lives, certain events and/or dates leave a mark. I still have not forgotten exactly what it felt like to wake up as a young girl to the record-breaking snowfall in Buffalo, NY during the blizzard of '77. Snow was not unusual in that part of the country, but having so much in such a little amount of time was a history maker. In fact, we had so much snow at our house that my brother had to jump out of the second story window just to be able to shovel up to our back door!

Another mark that comes to mind happened in the August of 1986...my first day at Stone Mountain High School. It was my freshman year, and we had just arrived the night before in Atlanta, GA. My mom had decided it was time for our family to make a change, so we uprooted from a small town and moved to the South. We had been a part of a small community my entire life, so that day first day of high school brought many emotions, both good and bad, because with my new school came many changes. My new school was more culturally diverse and about three times the size of my old one, and I had to ride a bus to school for the first time.

July 30, 1994 is another mark for me—my wedding day. As the bride, it was a day I had dreamed of for a long time. I remember the blue sky, the soft light in the sanctuary for our evening ceremony, and most of all, the look on Scott's face as I walked down the aisle. Having been married for nearly twenty-five years, this is a mark that will always be celebrated. Of course, there are lots of other dates— historical events, vacations, sporting events, college years, the birth of our kids, and many more. Still, some stick out more than others…they just leave a bigger mark. And if we let them, they begin to outline who we are. Somehow they influence or shape our identity. Some marks build a solid foundation, but others create cracks that allow our foundations to be weakened.

October 12, 1978 was a day that left a permanent mark. Some might describe it as a scar that never goes away. This was the day my dad told my brother and me that he was leaving my mom. He suffered from an addiction and was abusive, so the news was not surprising. Still, to an almost eight-year-old little girl, my world was shattered. That scar left such a big hole that I naturally tried to find something or someone to fill that gap. Even at that young age, rejection, abandonment, and little self-worth were all taking root and influencing my identity. My identity was being shaped by the choices others close to me were making.

We all try to fill the cracks in our foundation. Achievements, credentials, degrees, wins, likes, homes, jobs, kids, spouses, cars, friendships...all square pegs that don't fit the round holes. I certainly found myself trying to fit all of these things into the wide-open space left in my foundation created by my parents' divorce.

Thankfully, in the December of 1980 a lady named Mrs. Hobart left another mark—one that has brought Truth to my life. I received Christ at my personal Savior during a simple prayer at our church's AWANA meeting. A very broken ten-year-old girl saw God's love, hope, and kindness. He chose me even before I was born. At that time, I knew I needed Him more than ever. Nearly thirty-eight years later, I still feel the same way.

While I saw love and hope that day, the mark from my mom and dad's choice in 1978 still influenced many of my decisions, including how I saw others and events in my life. My fear of rejection and abandonment grew. My self-worth was often measured by what others said and did to me. I found myself making choices based on a wound that influenced almost every part of my being—emotional, spiritual and physical. This emotional wound began to take over and influence all aspects of my identity.

Identity is defined at dictionary.com as, "the qualities, beliefs, etc. that distinguish or identify a person or thing." My wound was influencing my feelings in such a way that my behaviors started to reflect the lies I believed about myself. This cocktail of lies I believed coupled with an unstable foundation brought a lot of unnecessary baggage into my marriage...baggage that I had been carrying for decades, not to mention I'd been picking up more along the way.

Then in September of 2017, another mark was made. I made another choice...a choice to learn how to approach my Heavenly Father for healing from those deep wounds that had influenced and shaped my identity. Through God's mercy and grace, He is "restoring the years that the locusts have eaten" to quote an Old Testament prophet. This has not been a quick or easy road. In fact, God and I have wrestled out many lies or beliefs that I had crafted in my own heart. Through some very influential Truth seekers, He has given me new tools to build a new foundation. I have seen the value of counseling, accountability, journaling, serving and giving. Though each of these, God continues to draw me close. He daily re-shapes my identity, which is built on His Truth of who I am in Him.

Day 14 Key Concept: Trust God's truth to define you

At times, I go through seasons where this choice is easy and things are good. Other times, I need to remind myself as soon as my feet hit the floor in the morning and say, "I am a daughter of The King. He loves me. He knows me. He values me. He wants me. He sees me. He chose me." In the Bible, we are reminded time and time again of God's love and desire for His people:

John 15:16 – *You did not choose me, but I chose you and appointed you so that you might go and bear fruit—fruit that will last—and so that whatever you ask in my name the Father will give you. (NIV)*

When I think back over my life, remembering the mark of my wedding day still brings lots of joy to this day. I am very thankful that God knit my husband and me together. While we are different in many ways—quiet and loud, tall and short, hot drinks and cold drinks—God brought us together to leave a legacy, one built on a firm foundation, and to pass a legacy onto our three boys. You do not need to let the choices of others shape who you are. Choose Him! He has already chosen you.

A Next Step:

For most of us, there are parts of our past that we would like to forget. Some may want to eliminate it altogether. Yet, our past shapes our present. Are there parts of your past that you have prayed through that continue to bring guilt or shame in your life? God's Word says that even when our hearts condemn us, God is greater than our hearts. Pray today and ask God if there are past events that you need to deal with and create a next step if needed.

_____

_____

_____

_____

_____

_____

_____

_____

_____

_____

_____

_____

_____

_____

_____

_____

_____

_____

_____

_____

_____

_____

_____

DAY 15
SEX & MEN

*How Divinity, Masculinity, and
Sexuality Work Together*

– Mike D.

(And my kids thought I embarrassed them **BEFORE**
I wrote this.)

This coming summer will mark the twenty-fifth
wedding anniversary for my wife and me. In an effort
to "keep it real," we tell people that we'll be celebrat-
ing about 23 ½ years of wedded bliss. Our marriage
has evolved and grown over the years. We've become
seasoned, and we've learned things—mostly through
our own mistakes. In those twenty-five years, our
marriage has had both peaks and valleys, but mostly
peaks.

My wife and I both grew up in Christian homes and in fairly conservative churches. While talking about sex wasn't as taboo as it is in some churches and families, it still wasn't a huge topic of conversation in our homes. We didn't learn much about sex at church, which isn't God's design because He wants married believers to enjoy the gift of sex and use it to draw closer to one another. (If you don't believe me, reread the Song of Solomon.) It's amazing how many Christian couples have told us that they have not prioritized sex in their marriage and failed to honor it the way God intended. With that in mind, my wife and I sensed God's pressing us to lead a Bible study written by Dr. Gary and Barbara Rosberg called *The 5 Sex Needs of Men and Women*. Through that study, we came to learn that sex is often more about attitude and emotion than it is about the physical act itself. Let me give you one example.

Early in our marriage, we had full-time jobs but no money. I spent four nights a week taking evening law school classes, which meant that we didn't get to spend much time together during the week. Nonetheless, we made it our mission to "keep the honeymoon rolling" as best we could. We'd received a book called *100 Nights of Great Sex* as a wedding gift. As you might expect, the book contained 100 ideas for spicing up a married couple's sex life. Some of the ideas were good…some were not. During one of our "valley" periods, my wife decided that we needed one of those 100 nights, so she opened the book and picked the first thing she saw. She was instructed to create a scavenger hunt map with clues that would lead her husband to the "treasure," which of course would be her...all wrapped up. However, since we lived in a very small house, she didn't have anywhere to hide. So, she did what any good wife would do. She waited until I was due home and snuck out to our outdoor shed where she finished getting the setting just right. There she was...X marked the spot of her husband's treasure hunt... all wrapped up. This would have been a great idea had her husband not been an idiot.

I was hungry, so after a full day's work and classes, I stopped on the way home to get something to eat. When I finally got home, I noticed the lights were mostly off and assumed that my wife had gotten tired and gone to bed. Given that I'd already eaten, I broke routine and didn't bother to check the fridge for my plated dinner, which is where the first clue was placed. Instead, I plopped down on the couch and watched a show or two. Did I mention that it was fairly cold that evening?!?! After waiting for me to find her for quite some time, my nearly hypothermic wife decided something was wrong and perhaps I wasn't coming to find her. Unfortunately, she had wrapped herself too well and wasn't able to move. I finally got tired, turned off the TV, and went to check the backdoor lock when I heard a muffled cry for help coming from our backyard. As you might expect, that was NOT one of our top 100 nights of great sex after all! While the evening didn't go as planned, my wife's effort to show me that she still cared about our intimate life was much appreciated, and it put us back on track.

The better your attitude is about sex and the more you understand how emotion impacts your partner, the more likely it is that you'll go way beyond the 100 nights promised in the book. Like most men, mutual sexual satisfaction is high on my list when it comes to sexual needs. Rosberg says, "Husbands want their wives to enjoy intimacy as much or more than the husbands actually do." That is to say, the more satisfied my wife is with our love life, the more I enjoy our relationship. The problem is that most men are never told what makes women enjoy sex. We think that their satisfaction is purely a physical thing. The culture hints to us that growing a thick mustache, buying special gadgets, and becoming a deliveryman are surely keys to satisfying women. Did it feel good or not? That's about as far as we go sometimes. Of course, the physical aspects of sex are not to be overlooked, but they are often useless if your wife isn't mentally engaged. My wife is not unlike most women in that affirmation is high on her list of sexual needs. In other words, she needs to know that she is still important and beautiful in my eyes. She needs to know that I value her as more than just a physical partner or someone to prepare a dinner each evening. She needs to know that she's appreciated, that connecting with her is valuable to me, and that our intimacy goes beyond our marriage bed. It's very important that I actually tell her these things and mean them. (She can tell the difference!) The need for affirmation is not only emotional. Our wives need to know that we still think they're hot, no matter how long we've been married or how rough the week has been. We even see this declaration of a man admiring his bride's beauty in Scripture:

Song of Solomon 4:1 – *Behold, you are beautiful, my love, behold, you are beautiful!*

By the way, two minutes before initiating intimacy isn't the only time to remind them how hot they are! Making sure to affirm our attraction to them throughout the week and providing them with "non-sexual" touches go a long way.

Day 15 Key Concept: For men and women, sex is more than just a physical act

Both men and women need connection to make sure their sex lives don't get displaced in the effort to keep up with all of their countless responsibilities. It's very important to show that you are both still a priority to each other. You have to be diligent to set aside time to reconnect. Sometimes, it can be a simple as having a lunch date. Sometimes you might need to plan a long (kid-free), romantic weekend. That said, please don't be intimidated by the incorrect notion that every "connection" has to be super romantic or perfect. Life is crazy, so sometimes you just have to make use of the time you get. You might even have to put "connection" on the schedule. When I still lived at home, my parents were adamant about my sister and me attending Sunday evening youth group meetings. I was always impressed by how much of a priority my dad placed on my spiritual discipleship, especially on Sunday nights. Years later, I connected the dots. (Can I get a collective, "Eeewww"?) The idea is that you have to be consistent in your effort to keep sex and connection a priority. The phrase "use it or lose it" should come to mind.

I want to share a caution with men, both married and single. For the most part, God created men with a strong, almost primal desire for sexual satisfaction—the physical part of sex. It's simply part of us. As Christians, it's very important that we satisfy this desire through our relationships with our wives and not elsewhere. In a world of Internet access and countless options, many men choose pornography as an easy alternative for sexual satisfaction. If you are single, just remember that you are not waiting on a physical act called sex. Rather, you are waiting on a person to marry. You can honor her in the future by the choices you make today. If you are married, it's much easier to click your way to satisfaction than to put in the necessary work to make sure your wife is satisfied with your marriage and sex life. Please don't take the easy way out. Know that pornography is infectious, even in otherwise strong Christian marriages. When a husband replaces marital sex with pornography, he often stops caring about the affirmation, connection, and intimacy his wife needs. She, in turn, stops making an effort sexually. This creates the proverbial death spiral in their marriage. This is as much a caution to women as it is to men. Please know that if your husband seems to be no longer interested in intimacy, you should have an honest discussion with him. Men don't often just lose interest in sex; many times, they are filling that void

in a way that is not healthy. Prioritize your sexual
relationship inside of the context of your marriage...
it's a gift that God has given to us.

A Next Step:

It's been said that a man's greatest need is respect
and a woman's greatest need is love. Men, how can
how you show love today to your spouse? If you
are single, how can you show her that you care
for and respect her as God's daughter? If you are
married, how can you let your wife know that she
is more important than your physical needs?

_____

_____

_____

_____

_____

_____

_____

_____

_____

_____

_____

_____

DAY 16

THE KNOCK ON YOUR DOOR THAT NO ONE WANTS TO ANSWER

God & Grieving

– Darwin & Stephanie M.

All it takes is one knock on your door to send your once perfect world crashing into a million pieces.

In 1997, Darwin and I were married, and like many couples, we chose 1 Corinthians 13 as one of our readings:

1 Corinthians 13:13 – *And now these three remain: faith, hope, and love. But the greatest of these is love. (NIV)*

These verses seemed fitting, not only because we had heard this same reading at pretty much every other wedding we'd been to, but because that's a couple's story. Faith in each other, hope that it all works out, and getting married because we are ridiculously in love.

Love has been our story. We have been fortunate to have so many blessings throughout our twenty years of marriage. We have two wonderful daughters, Hunter and Reese, a nice house, good friends, and enough money to be comfortable enough to take vacations. Sure, we have gone through difficult times, particularly when Darwin lost his father and then his brother a few years later to Leukemia. We also have dealt with the stressors that come with family life, raising two children, and working full-time jobs. When those times hit, we worked together to carry the burden, fifty-fifty. Still, it had been pretty smooth sailing.

Through it all, God was there. Not front-and-center, in-your-face there, but always a Presence. We liked God, appreciated all of His gifts, went to church on Sundays, and said prayers before meals and bedtime. We taught our girls that it was important to be nice to others, use good manners, and listen to their elders. You know, Christian things. It was working, too. Our girls were doing well in school, had great friends, and were usually pretty delightful to be around. We were a happy family.

On July 17, 2017, everything we knew about life changed in an instant. We got that knock on our door.

Our seventeen-year-old daughter, Hunter, was killed in a car accident as a passenger, and everything we thought we knew about marriage, family, life, and God were turned upside down. I had always heard that God wouldn't give you more than you can handle. Nowhere in the Bible does it say that, and clearly this statement is a myth, because I knew with every fiber of my being that I was not going to be able to handle my daughter's death on my own. Instead, I needed to turn to what was actually in the Bible.

Philippians 4:13 – *For I can do everything through Christ, who gives me strength. (NLT)*

Darwin and I had to embrace this truth and press into God—this was going to be the difference in whether or not we endured Hunter's loss.

In the beginning, we needed strength just to get out of bed each morning. As we continued to rely on God, He continued to give us the strength to make it through her birthday, Thanksgiving, Christmas, and her would-be graduation.

Let me be very clear here: neither does our faith in God nor eternity make this remotely easy, but they do make it possible. Every day is a battle for our family. Our grief is all consuming, and we walk around with a child-sized hole in our hearts that no one can fill. We could be tempted to live the rest of our lives in fear, doubt, anger, and self-pity, which could send us spiraling into a deep dark pit that we could never climb out of. Instead, we have chosen to pursue God. We make a conscious, intentional choice to seek

Him daily and even moment-by-moment at times. For us, this has meant going to a Christian-based support group, reading book upon book about faith and Heaven, putting Bible verses up throughout our house, listening to worship music, and surrounding ourselves with other believers whose faith and prayers have kept us going when we were running low. We continue going to church and end each day by climbing into bed together, holding hands, and praying. We pray for strength to get through the next moment, for comfort, and for a peace that surpasses all understanding. We pray that we would keep our eyes fixed on Christ and to have an eternal perspective. Finally, we pray for protection for our family and our marriage.

We've also had to realize that each of us grieves in our own way. Darwin and I have had to be willing to talk—really talk—about how to handle the different situations that came our way. While we sometimes agreed, we had to respect and understand that we weren't going to necessarily see eye-to-eye throughout the grief process. We were always there for each other, but we also had to give each other space at times. Communication, always a key to a successful marriage, became even more important in our grief. Darwin and I have been blessed to have a strong marriage, but we also know that losing a child is one of the most difficult and traumatic events a couple can go through. We are committed to each other more than ever, and we vow that our younger daughter, who has already lost her sister, will not lose her mom and dad to this tragedy too.

Looking back to that young couple who said their vows with a bright future ahead of them, it's hard to believe where we are now. Still, 1 Corinthians 13 holds true—even today. What we've come to realize is that the verse is not about Darwin and me, but about God and us.

On our refrigerator, I taped phrases I'd seen in a book because I wanted to make sure we read it every day. It has become our daily creed:

We believe that God's promises are true.

We believe Heaven is real and Hunter is there waiting for us.

We believe nothing can separate us from God's love.

We believe God has work for us to do.

We believe God will carry us when we cannot walk.

Faith, hope, and love are at the center of this creed. Having faith and trusting God and His promises help us get through each day. Our hope lies in His promises, and the promise of being reunited with Hunter one day. We know that this world and our pain are not the end. God loves us so much that He sent Jesus. Through his sacrifice on the cross, our spirits live on for eternity. We also know that God loves us because He gave us Hunter for seventeen years, and our faith tells us that she is waiting for us—she is a treasure we have stored up in Heaven. Our faith and hope in God and His love will carry us through anything we experience on this earth, until we are together rejoicing in Heaven.

We wish this wasn't our story. We'd be happier writing about anything else having to do with marriage and family, but unfortunately this is our story. It's the one we have to tell now, and though it's difficult, we can also confidently say that it's a story about God's love. In addition to everything else, God has given us these words:

1 Thessalonians 4:13 – *Brothers and sisters, we do not want you to be uninformed about those who sleep in death, so that you do not grieve like the rest of mankind, who have no hope. (NIV)*

Day 16 Key Concept: Let God's love guide you through your grief

A Next Step:

Many people experience loss, but the loss of a child is unique. It's life out of order. Sometimes, as families or individuals experience this kind of loss, the immediate uprising of care is like a huge mega-wave that can be followed by what feels like a sinkhole. Who are folks that you know, who've experienced this kind of loss? Over time, what creative ways can you consider to appropriately recognize their loss and minister to them?

_____

_____

_____

_____

_____

_____

_____

_____

_____

_____

_____

_____

_____

_____

_____

_____

_____

_____

_____

_____

_____

_____

_____

_____

_____

DAY 17
JUST SAY SO

*How to Trust God to Speak Truth
into Your Relationship*

– Cindy & Bryan M.

Quite a few years ago, we packed up our family and headed to a beach house in the Carolinas to enjoy some time away. We had a great week enjoying the sun, sand, and one another. One evening, Bryan made a little comment as I was getting dinner ready. He observed, out loud, that there had to be a better way to cut the pineapple than the method I was using. I considered the remark to be an all-out assault on my ability to care for my family (Okay, that's an exaggeration, but the comment did sting). Rather than speaking "now or forever holding my peace," I chose to remain silent but harbored resentment.

I put the comment on a running list I had in my head of the ways Bryan obviously believed that I was a terrible wife and mom. I didn't ask God to give me courage to be honest in the moment, and I certainly didn't trust that God would be in the mess, if I spoke up.

Like most things that are hidden, it couldn't stay hidden forever. So, two months after our vacation, Bryan and I had a big ol' fight over…wait for it… pineapple cutting! Today, I laugh when I remember the look of utter shock on Bryan's face when I finally revealed why I'd been so distant since we'd returned from the beach—all over fruit cutting methods!

We jokingly refer to the incident as the "pineapple thing," but that moment paints a crystal clear picture of how Bryan and I tend to go wrong, when it comes to communication. We have a trust problem.

Day 17 Key Concept: Our communication problem isn't that we don't trust our *spouse* enough to be honest—we don't trust *God* enough to put our marriage in His hands

Time and again, God has made it known to us through Scripture that He both designed marriage and is for our marriage.

Mark 10:6-9 – *But at the beginning of creation, "God made them male and female." "Therefore a man shall leave his father and mother and hold fast to his wife, and the two shall become one flesh." So they are no longer two but one flesh. What therefore God has joined together, let not man separate.*

God is so whole-heartedly for our marriage that He inexplicably takes two completely separate people with their own personalities, traits, self-interests, and sinful desires, and He transforms them into one. If we believe this, then we are free to be honest with our spouses, even with issues bigger than how we slice up fruit. We can have confidence that God will deliver us from the messes we make, because He will both empower us to forgive and grant us the courage to ask for forgiveness. He will give us words and wisdom to navigate the sticky, painful situations we find ourselves in so often in marriage. He will heal the wounds we unintentionally inflict and teach us over time how to be more tender with each other.

But when it comes to honesty, some may wonder if it's it ever okay to withhold a secret from your spouse? To put it another way, "Do I have to tell my spouse everything?" What if I know that what I'm about to say will really hurt them? What if I think we could get a divorce over the information I am withholding? These are tough questions, but our experience has been that being totally honest has been the best course—even when we knew it could hurt. While there may be small exceptions to this (for example, if you're telling your spouse something out of spite or revenge), we owe it to our spouses to reveal our innermost thoughts, feelings, and desires.

When deciding what to communicate to each other, we like to ask a few additional questions:

1. Is this issue causing me to be distant from my spouse or to build up resentment?

2. Would my spouse be devastated if they found
    out from someone else?

If the answer is "yes" to either of these questions,
then we tell each other. We remind ourselves that
we must trust God with our marriage and that He
desires the best for us. Even though our comments
might initially sting, we believe that through prayer
and God's grace, He will heal our wounds. We also
believe that our marriage is stronger, because we
can be confident that neither of us has anything
left to hide.

After seven years of dating and nearly twenty
years of marriage, it appears as though communication is not something we will master anytime
soon. But God is with us, and we are grateful. He
will fill in the gaping holes we make in the fabric of
our marriage. We know He will because His word
reveals that His design is that we would become one.

As we stumble along, here is what we do with
those truths in mind:

1. **We pray together**, thanking God for the
    miracle of making two one, and we expec-
    tantly listen to His leading in our marriage.
    It is very surprising how many couples we
    have talked with who do not pray together.
    Bringing each other into our communication
    with God by praying together has probably
    been the most important step we've taken
    together as a couple.

2. **We are honest** about our past (this one
    was tough), our feelings, our needs, and our

desires. We realize that many people may have pasts that include previous partners, sexual sin, addiction, and many other issues, so this point should not be taken lightly. We used a resource called "Steps to Freedom in Christ" that walked us through the process of praying through our past. We would recommend talking through this process with a pastor or counselor first.

3. **We examine our motivation** for what we communicate to each other. Philippians 2:3 states, "Do nothing out of selfish ambition or vain conceit. Rather, in humility value others above yourselves." Any communication we have with each other is intended to build up our marriage or each other.

Finally, the proper way to slice a pineapple is... whatever way she wants to slice it!

A Next Step:

Very few people enjoy hard conversations. They require us to admit our own wrong in many cases. As you consider having a difficult meeting, recognize your own conflict default. Almost everyone has a "fight" or a "flight" mentality. You have to work against your natural tendency at times. Go into the conversation with a willingness to listen and learn, as opposed to listening and defending.

DAY 18

DEALING WITH DIVORCE

What to Do When You Don't Know What to Do

– Louise B.

It's a word I never thought I'd hear personally. But after over twenty-nine years of marriage, it described me—divorced. Although it was a surprise to me, my children, and my family and friends, it was not a surprise to God. God would use this in my life in so many ways.

What I realized in the months of my separation and divorce was that I had made my husband, my marriage, and my family into an idol. I had put my husband above God. I had put my marriage above God. Please don't misunderstand me. I know and believe marriage is wonderful, it's a blessing, and it's a good thing. However, putting marriage above God was wrong. My identity was in my "Mrs." title, and then it was suddenly gone. I am learning that God wants me to put Him first in my life and desires me to live in the reality that I am deeply loved.

It's not been easy. I've discovered that when going through a separation or a divorce, the enemy will attack, attack, and then attack again. He loves to remind me that I was failure at my marriage, and I wasn't loveable, attractive enough, smart enough, or desirable enough. Then comes the dagger...that I would spend the rest of my life alone. As a result, fear and fear and some more fear set in. Honestly, the list could go on about the darkness I experienced. I can tell you that I reached the lowest point in my life during those months when my marriage was falling apart. The pain was so unbearable that there were times when I just wanted the pain to stop; I just wanted my life to be over.

But God...

Despite the many dark days, God consistently reminded me that I was loved, that I was needed, and that He wasn't done with me. I kept hearing from God the words of Deuteronomy 31:6 that, "He will not leave you or forsake you." God blessed and blessed and blessed some more. He met me in those dark, lonely places every single time. During the darkness, a friend would call or send a text. Often a worship song would come on to lift up my heart, or I would read something in His word (the Psalms are amazing) or in a devotional, and it would be what I needed to hear. Other times, one of my children would want to hang out with me.

Through it all, God was and is working in me and in my family. One way I know is because the spiritual warfare has been ramped up. Still, we have all the tools we need to fight the enemy. Even though the enemy likes to remind us of our past, of our failures, and of our hurts and shame, we can fight back by reminding him that he has already been defeated by what Jesus did on the Cross. The enemy has no future! While the enemy will try to increase your pain, cling to the biblical truths about who you are and where your future really lies.

Even so, divorce comes with so many losses... loss of a mate, a marriage, your identity, dreams of a future, retirement together, sharing future grandchildren, extended family, a home, income. Thankfully, I can say:

But God...

God has provided for me in so many ways.

Day 18 Key Concept: God is always at work

In the end, my best piece of advice is to lean into Jesus. I still remember the dark days, but I don't recall them with sadness. Instead, I remember them as the times when God met me exactly where I was. He never let me down—not once. On days when I didn't think I could make it through, I did. There were some days when I literally got by hour by hour. Through this experience, I've learned that I want to have that desperate need for God every day. I don't want to do it on my own anymore. I want more—more of God, more of His peace, His love, His forgiveness, His grace, His mercy.

My prayer each day is from Ezekiel:

Ezekiel 36:26 – *And I will give you a new heart, and I will put a new spirit in you. I will take out your stony, stubborn heart and give you a tender, responsive heart. (NLT)*

There are other verses that I've been clinging to during this season. I keep hearing from God, "I will never leave you or forsake you" (Deuteronomy 31:6), and "Be still and know that I am God" (Psalm 46:10). Finally, God's word reminds me that He is always working on my behalf:

John 5:17 – *Jesus replied, "My Father is always working, and so am I." (NLT)*

When I am tempted to take back control of a certain area of my life, these verses come to mind. I don't want to be in control anymore. I don't know what my future holds. I don't know if my marriage will ever be reconciled, if God will bring along someone else, or if God will allow me to be single the rest of my life. Whatever my future holds, God is already there. He is still in the miracle business, and He promises redemption and reconciliation. My entire life, I've been a "Daddy's Girl" with my earthly father. Now I can say, "I'm a Daddy's Girl" with my Heavenly Father. I can live with that identity.

A Next Step:

While it's certainly becoming less common in Christianity, people who have been through a divorce can feel like they wear a Scarlet letter. This can result in feelings of failure, guilt, and shame. The Body of Christ should be a place where we constantly remind each other that ALL of us are flawed. In your life, how could you specifically reach out to someone who has experienced divorce? Maybe it could be connected to a special holiday or birthday.

_____

_____

_____

_____

_____

_____

_____

_____

_____

_____

_____

_____

_____

_____

_____

_____

_____

DAY 19
GOING FORWARDS BACKWARDS

How God Can Restore Relationships
– Linda & John H.

"Unless the LORD builds the house, those who build it labor in vain." Psalm 127:1

"Laboring in vain" could've been my epitaph! I was OCD before the term even existed. Everything I did had to be 100%, A-plus, 10-level work. Whether it was a homework assignment or simply a household chore, I did it to perfection—meanwhile driving everyone around me perfectly insane. As high school sweethearts, that was acceptable to my significant other. However, as a young wife, it was anything but okay. After ten years of marriage, my husband, John, was totally miserable. When his printing business lost its three biggest clients, he was forced to close it down permanently. Desperate to start life over, he felt everything had to change in his life—everything—that is, except for the love he had for his two daughters. So, in 1980 he left me swearing never to return, but he promised to keep in touch with our two girls.

I was devastated. All my life, I'd been a strong Catholic. I always followed every rule to the max. I even added some of my own! Looking back, I knew all about God, and yet I didn't really know Him at all!

Forced to sell everything we owned, I thought I had nowhere to go and no one to turn to for help. All I wanted was to get my family back together again, but it looked hopeless. That's when a friend suggested I accompany her to a Bible study.

I. Was. Livid.

Who was she to tell me about God? But I was desperate. I went and for the first time in my life, I heard the Gospel for the first time. However, I left that woman's home in utter disbelief. How could anyone claim to know that they were "saved" and going to Heaven? Who in the world could be sure that they were forgiven and that God would never leave them? The audacity to be that sure of a relationship with God!

After two weeks of immense turmoil, I called the woman back, and she led me to Christ. Ever since, nothing has been the same. Sure, my life was a still a total mess. My husband was gone, and the girls and I had to leave our home, sell almost everything we had, and move into an apartment. I had to get a job outside the home, and the girls had to adjust to all these changes. But now, God was in the picture!

For seven years, John had daily contact with the girls but rarely spoke to me. Through one miracle after another, God took care of us...financially, physically, emotionally, and spiritually. Most of all, during that time, God showed us that He was not a distant, far away Presence, but a kind and loving Father who cares about even the smallest details in our lives.

After a short time, the girls accepted Christ, and we all began attending a Bible teaching church. The girls never missed an opportunity to share Jesus with John, but he thought this was yet another of my crazy tangents. One day, the girls told him they'd been offered a scholarship to attend a Christian school, but he was angry and even threatened to take the girls away from me. As a result, I prayed for many days about it and finally submitted to his "requests," but I wanted the girls to be exposed to Scripture as much as possible. After four years of separation, John filed for and received a divorce, even though I didn't even show up in court. I'd decided that Jesus had brought us this far, and He would take care of the details. Trusting Jesus was the only real security we had in our lives. He was faithful and always provided us with a loving family, Christian pastors, and godly friends.

Day 19 Key Concept: Build your home on the foundation of Christ

At the time, our pastor was Jim Custer, and during one Sunday sermon he suggested that we pray for those in our lives who were deeply hurting us. Even more, we should ask God to shower them with His goodness and grace. (Until then my favorite prayer for John was a Psalm: "I will contend with those who contend with you!") I decided to give it a try. Soon after, John got a great job and started earning a better living. To me, life seemed great for him. He moved us into a nice home and even took the kids on a Florida vacation. When they were in Florida, the girls begged John to give me a second chance, and his response was a resounding, "NO!"

Then, the unimaginable happened. Later that summer, a potential client agreed to come to town to meet with John. However, the client would only come if he could attend a Bible teaching church on the Sunday he was in town. Ironically, the only church John could think of was the one the girls and I attended. Imagine my surprise when I saw him sitting there in church. I could only marvel at what God had done.

As only God could orchestrate, on that particular Sunday our pastor chose to preach about divorce. He explained that divorce wasn't the issue, but the real problem was having a hardened heart towards Jesus. That afternoon, John came over, and we talked. Five months later, we were remarried in our garage. John even accepted Jesus before our wedding and has grown into a godly father, husband, and leader.

That was over thirty years, two sons-in-law, and six grandkids ago!

Is life perfect? I'll answer that by quoting what my daughter, Lori, said to Pastor Dean when he asked us to write this chapter: "Are you sure you have the right family?" Nothing on this earth will ever be perfect, but there is one thing I've learned. When the Lord builds a house, it might not be easy. It's almost always challenging. But the labor is never, ever in vain. (By the way, both of our daughters now serve at the Christian school they weren't allowed to attend, and all six of our grandchildren have been blessed by being students there as well).

I know that your path may be different than ours. It may have a different ending. But if you're walking with the Lord, He will always be faithful to you, and you'll always end up right where you belong. Not everyone receives the happy ending on this earth that our family eventually found. Our family still has challenges. But we never feel alone.

A Next Step:

Throughout life, relationships of various kinds can come and go for many reasons. Today, take a moment to pray for someone in your life with whom you no longer have much contact. Pray that the person would have a deep knowledge of God. Ask God if there is someone you need to reach out to.

DAY 20

IMPERFECTLY PERFECT

When Super-Christians Learn Surrender

– Rachelle A.

"Then they sweep by like the wind and go on, guilty men, whose own might is their god."
Habakkuk 1:11

To determine the moments of greatest influence in life, we often go straight to the waterfall experiences—the spectacular, powerful, waterfall events that carve a deep chasm into the soil of our lives. But there is something to be said about the spigot. The spigot is the faucet on the outside of the house. No one thinks twice about it, but the spigot drips. All winter long, a steady drip changes the dirt below, and something is carved without anyone noticing.

All hail the waterfall, but let's not underestimate the power of the spigot.

I was my dad's daughter. People often told me how lucky I was to have such a wise, godly father who brought many people to Jesus. As a child, I basked in his value, feeling my worth in his. My parents were in Christian ministry, but not the kind with a steady paycheck. It was the raise your own support kind, and money was a source of stress for my parents and also for me. I felt shame in this. On the one hand, I was proud to be my dad's daughter. On the other, I was ashamed by what was happening behind the scenes…we didn't have enough money to make our world go round.

I was also my mamma's daughter. She seemed perfect. She loved Jesus, and her life's mission was loving other people. She was beautiful, always put together, and expected my sister and I to be put together too. Mamma grew up in a home with no stability, so in her own home, she controlled the environment to be just how she wanted. She craved perfection, and by default, her daughters felt the need to be perfect too.

Growing up, I experienced lots of love and lots of Jesus. By all Christian standards, my parents did it the right way. They followed God's call for their lives. They valued their relationship and modeled biblical marriage by serving each other. They invested intentionally in my sister and me. By all accounts, my parents gave me the idyllic childhood. Still, I reached out and grabbed onto something very different than what they showed.

At some point, I gobbled down the lie that my value was in my perfection and my worth was in my doing. I felt no freedom to fail. As a result, I covered up anything less than stellar about me. My deception was that instead of disappointing my parents with the truth, I handed them pleasing white lies.

There was no waterfall defining moment in my childhood that fueled this thinking and led to my horrific failures as an adult. I certainly never set out to make my own strength my god. But when I look at the mistakes I've made in adulthood, I have to go back to that spigot, which was dripping a sorry kind of truth about where my value lay. Unfortunately, these lies didn't automatically turn off when I reached adulthood.

As an adult, I believed my value was in my perfection. Self-inflicted pressure drove every area of my life, and to involve myself in something was to become obsessed with mastery. This included my relationship with Jesus. I attended Bible studies, led Bible studies, served the least of these, homeschooled my own children, and by all appearances was a super Christian. I did for God. My knowledge of God, zeal for God, and "should do" mentality seemed to power my Christian walk just fine. But as it turns out, when our own strength empowers the Christian life, that Christian life has no real power at all.

My self-inflicted pressure to be the best at everything suffocated me. I needed escape and found it in alcohol. A seemingly well-deserved glass of wine each night soon became the nightly numbing needed to survive my "perfect" life. The pressure disappeared but an addiction grew, and so did deceit as my secret life raged.

Then, it happened. On a cold day in February, God chased me down and set me free. A Power beyond me interrupted my life and shattered the chains of alcohol—I was miraculously healed from my addiction. In the wake of receiving a rescue I didn't even want, I knew without a doubt that God had healed me. Still, the experience left me quite broken. I felt exposed. I had to face the truth of what I was. Even more, I had to face the truth about what God wasn't.

The painful truth was this: what I had of Jesus hadn't been enough for me. All my Bible knowledge and Christian efforts didn't satisfy my soul. I wondered if "super-Christian" me didn't find Jesus to be enough for the pressure and pain of living, then how could He be possibly be enough? If I couldn't be satisfied in Him, who could be? Something was lost in translation between my dutiful morning devotion and my nightly numbing.

I began slinging hard questions to the God of the Universe. I began reading the Bible like it was actually supposed to be true. John 10:10 says that Jesus came to give me abundant living. I certainly wasn't experiencing this so-called abundant living, so I had to wonder, "Does Jesus really give it? If so, how can I find it?"

I read through Acts and was astounded by the power of the Holy Spirit who transformed fearful Jesus followers to fearless saints who revolutionized the world. I wondered if that same Holy Spirit who gave power to the weak was the same Holy Spirit in me today? God says He is, but where was the Holy Spirit? Why couldn't I discern His voice, let alone experience His transformational power?

Isaiah 30:15 tells us, "In repentance and rest you will be saved, in quietness and trust is your strength', but you were not willing." That sounded familiar. But how was strength and salvation found in the quiet? Laced throughout Scripture is the consistent thread of humbling yourself before God, but how? My thirty-five years of Christianity had been about doing, and I didn't know how to receive from God without driving the effort. But I decided to take Isaiah 30:15 as truth and asked God to show me how to be quiet before Him. As a result, God taught me the hardest thing I've ever learned—He taught me how to be still. In stillness, He began to speak. And in speaking, He wooed me to surrender.

In surrender, I found Power. I found something beyond my Christian effort and knowledge. I found a mind-blowing, overwhelming, holy God. In quieting myself before Him, God began to show me glimpses of Himself. I was overwhelmed by God's holiness. However, gazing into the truth about God soon revealed the truth about me. For the first time ever in my years of following Jesus, I realized I had quite a sin problem. My problem went far beyond the obvious sins of addiction and deceit. I was ridden with lurking, hidden sins, so attached to my life that they almost looked like my personality. Comparison and jealousy. Vanity and obsession with my look. A critical and judgmental spirit towards my husband. Unforgiveness. Pride. The list goes on and on. I began to understand that sin is a big deal.

Yes, as a Christian, my sin is paid for by the death of Jesus. Still, sin grieves God. Sin keeps me from hearing the whispers of the Holy Spirit, and it can still destroy my life.

The Holy Spirit gently exposed my sin and then set me free from my bondage to sin. I learned that the Holy Spirit is not an accessory to Christian living; He is Christian living. Jesus died on the cross, rose from the dead, went back to Heaven, and sent the Holy Spirit to power our lives. Unfortunately, we super-Christians have the tendency to make our own strength our God. Humans can power their Christianity, but when we do, our Christianity has no real power. The abundant living that Jesus came to give us is not found in human power.

Abundant living is simply this: it is living by God's power. To experience abundant living, we must surrender. All Christians have the Holy Spirit, but not all Christians live surrendered to the Holy Spirit. Surrender means offering God control of my life. It's laying down my will and asking for His. It's laying down my power and asking for His. When we do this, He gives us more than we ask or imagine.

Day 20 Key Concept: The abundant life is found in surrender

Jesus followers cannot have it both ways. We cannot power our lives and expect to know God's power. It is impossible to be filled with the fullness of God and be filled to the brim with our own egos. It is in our emptiness that God fills us. It is in our surrender that we gain His power. Through His power, we experience abundant living. It is in abundant living, as His truth replaces ours, when we can finally turn off that spigot.

A Next Step:

Sometimes, in an honest desire to live a life of obedience to God, we can begin to think that our standing before God and His love towards us depends upon our actions. Our good intentions can easily distort the Gospel and leave us believing lies about God and ourselves. Take a moment to pray and ask God to help you see if you are trying to live out the Christian life through His power or your own. Pray and ask God to help you live a life surrendered to Him.

_____

_____

_____

_____

_____

_____

_____

_____

_____

DAY 21

STIRRING THE RIGHT STUFF

Modern Day Experiences for Old School Values

– Shane & Ellen T.

Shane and I couldn't have had more different sibling relationships when we were young. Shane had a close bond with his older brother Bobby. They would sneak into each other's rooms at night and stay up late talking and laughing. Bobby would frequently let Shane hang out with him and his friends even though it would've been very easy for Bobby to exclude him. The two had each other's back and were incredibly close.

I also had an older brother, plus a younger sister. Unfortunately, we weren't as close and too many of my memories involve us bickering, fighting, and hurting one another's feelings. I always knew I wanted something different for my own children but had no idea how to make that happen.

After the birth of our third child, Shane and I stumbled upon a book that helped us create an action plan for building a healthy family. As we waded through this process, we realized that we aren't the only ones with an agenda for our children's lives. The world offers plenty of distractions that threaten to steer our children away from our family, from God, and from our values. As God's Word reveals, parents are instrumental in laying a foundation for their children's faith:

Proverbs 22:6 – *Train up a child in the way he should go; even when he is old he will not depart from it.*

We've decided we will do whatever we can to raise our children in such a way that they will not depart from the Lord. We're aware that many of our childhood friends from youth group have left the church and now reject God. This is exactly what we want to avoid! We desire to raise a generation who runs toward God, not away from Him. We also realize the world offers much to steer our children off the path, so our desire is to make our family's values more attractive, more real, and more significant than the world's temptations.

But how do we do that? How do we root our children in what God values? God shows us the right direction in Scripture:

Deuteronomy 6:6-9 – *And these words that I command you today shall be on your heart. You shall teach* *them diligently to your children, and shall talk of them when you sit in your house, and when you walk by the way, and when you lie down, and when you rise. You shall bind them as a sign on your hand, and they shall be as frontlets between your eyes. You shall write them on the doorposts of your house and on your gates.*

In Deuteronomy, we see the importance of sharing God's commands with our children. In fact, the writer stresses the need to drill God's laws and promises into our children's daily lives and memories. Now, let's face it: our memories fade and we easily forget. If it weren't for videos, we are pretty sure we would have no clue what our children's voices sounded like as toddlers. And that's our very own children! How much easier is it to forget God's activity in our lives? If we want our children to know God, His promises, and how He is at work in our family, we have to be diligent and purposeful to talk about, read about, and experience Him.

So, we finally became purposeful in our parenting. We sat down and identified our core values and how we wanted our family to reflect Christ. We started to thoroughly explore what we could do to create a family dynamic that fostered our values: a love for the Lord and people, healthy sibling relationships, and fun and laughter. Along the way, it occurred to us that creating purposeful and beautiful family experiences could help our children desire our values.

After identifying our core values, we had to figure out how to build experiences around them. Our hope is that the physical actions, the experiences, will help them remember the underlying values. While young children don't know enough to care about a list of beliefs, they will remember the experiences we provide them.

Our next step was to gather our small group together and create a lengthy list of ideas that would help us move our family in the direction we wanted to go. Our desire is that by implementing these experiences, our children will grow up to remember, appreciate, and adhere to our values. If the awesome family memories our children have help point them to God, then we hope the effort we put into making memories helps our kids remember and love God's standards and resist the world's.

The experiences alone are fantastic, but remember how we have a memory problem? To make sure we could provide them with proof that we were purposeful (and fun-loving!) parents, we started recording our adventures and making videos for our children. Just as our Bibles or our prayer journals prompt us to remember what God has done, we know that we need to document our experiences so that our children would have physical reminders of what we value. We now have dozens of videos, and our children absolutely love watching them—on repeat! The videos prompt their memory, curiosity, and affections for one another.

Ultimately, we want our children to know that God truly loves them and for them to love Him back with everything they are. We hope that our attempts to create special moments will remind them of our love but—more importantly—remind them of God's love and stir up their affections for Christ.

Day 21 Key Concept: Help stir up your children's affections for Christ

We want to leave you with a web address to visit so you can see how we document our journey and perhaps encourage you to do the same: shanetucker. com/blog. Below are some ideas from our experience list in case you would want to implement some in your family. We found several of these ideas from Google searches, talking to friends, and Pinterest. Explore for yourself and find ideas that fit your family's values.

Memory Making Ideas:

Teach the Kids the Art of the Ding-Dong-Ditch
Take a Mission Trip Together
Organize a Water Balloon Fight
Host a Family Dance Contest
Buy Christmas Dinner or Groceries for a Stranger
Perform Random Acts of Kindness
Set up the Tent in the Living Room and Sleep in it
    Together
Write and Deliver Valentines
Plan a Family Date Night (Kid-Planned on a Budget)
Plan a Parent/Child Date Night
Donate Toys to Local Charities
Share a Formal Dinner at Wendy's (Table Cloth, Fancy
    Cups, Formal Attire)
Star Gaze on the Trampoline
Sweat Together in a Family Work Out
Create Obstacle Courses
Visit Garage Sales (Kids Get Their Own Money to
    Spend)

Complete a Family Puzzle
Serve Someone Together (Service Project)
Surprise the Kids with a Food Fight
Arrange an ATV Excursion

A Next Step:

Take some time to pinpoint your family's core values. What do you want your kids to leave your home believing and thinking about life? Next brainstorm some ideas for how you could create experiences in your children's lives to help them remember your family's core values. If you need a little help, reach out to your small group leader or children's pastor. You could also check out Lifepoint's Family Framework that gives four habits (Modeling, Meeting, Moments, and Milestones) to help develop a rhythm of family discipleship.

_____

_____

_____

_____

_____

_____

_____

_____

_____

_____

_____

_____

_____

_____

_____

_____

_____

_____

_____

_____

_____

_____

_____

_____

_____

_____

_____

_____

_____

_____

_____

_____

_____

_____

_____

DAY 22

WHEN YOUR CHILD HURTS

Learning to Give Thanks for It When You Are in It

– Carrie H.

Our son Toby is one of the bravest people I know. In almost twelve years of life, he's faced several life-threatening situations, as well as thirty-nine surgeries. He can't walk, has a trach tube to help him breathe, and depends on mechanical ventilation at night to keep him alive. My husband and I have seen him endure more pain and suffering than a room full of adults will ever experience in a lifetime. I've often heard others say, "He doesn't deserve that; no child deserves that." On the surface, that might be true, but through the years, our perspective on suffering and what we "deserve" or "don't deserve" has changed.

Raising a child with medical and special needs is like living on a sine curve. A sine curve has ups and downs. It has high points and lows. This is true of roller coasters or winding roads in the mountains.

During one particularly low part of our sine curve, I was really struggling. As a result of Toby's medical needs, we've always had private duty nursing care in our home. We can't leave him with a babysitter or with anyone who isn't trained to perform his medical care. Even normal activities that most couples do, such as going on dates or getting away for a night, have never been easy for us. Our children require a nurse AND a babysitter, and those nights away must be planned well in advance. In the middle of a time when nurses were scarce, I was praying and lamenting to the Lord about the difficulty of our situation. I remember thinking, "Lord, this is hard on us, and it's really hard on Toby. It's not fair to him to have all this inconsistency."

His response was not what I expected.

God spoke in my heart and said, "What if I have a reason for this? What if some of these nurses don't know Me? What if they are only in your home for one day because contact with your family causes them to look for Me? Is it worth it?"

I understood what He meant, but I was still wondering why my son had to suffer through all of this.

Again, His response wasn't what I expected.

"Did my own Son suffer? I'm a parent, too; do you know what I suffered when Jesus left heaven? He died a horrific death—one He did not deserve for a world not deserving of salvation. He was perfect, and He gave himself up for you and your son, for you to know Me—to truly know comfort and peace even in the middle of difficult circumstances and for you to experience hope."

The fact is we are sinners, and we deserve the worst—hell, death, and separation from God. But because God loves us so much, He sent Jesus to give us what we do not deserve: a relationship with Him and hope, comfort, and peace. We have hope that, no matter what happens, we have His power, His love, and Himself, the God of the universe, waiting for us in Heaven.

On this journey, when we face yet another low part on the sine curve, I sometimes ask God some of the same questions. Why is God requiring more of us…especially of Toby? But through His strength and power, He is growing our faith and drawing us closer to Him.

Day 22 Key Concept: In Christ, God always treats us better than we deserve

So, what are some practical ways we deal with having a child who suffers so much?

First of all, focus on today.

Matthew 6:34 – *Therefore do not worry about tomorrow, for tomorrow will worry about itself. Each day has enough trouble of its own. (NIV)*

One time, Toby had been in the hospital intensive care unit fighting for his life when I learned an important lesson about trust. It was very challenging for me, a "Type A Planner," not to have the next weeks and months planned out…to NOT know what the future held. Would Toby even be alive tomorrow? There were days I was hanging onto Jesus for each breath Toby took. Through this, God taught me that He holds tomorrow. No matter what happens, He is in control. And He can be trusted because He loves me. The Bible teaches that Christ's return is imminent and no one knows the day or the hour. I could spend all day fraught with worry when Jesus could return…tonight…in the next hour. All that worry would've been for nothing. So, I am learning to take each hour as just that hour. I'm asking God every morning for His mercies, strength, and love to flood my heart and give me peace just for that day. Francis de Sales said, "Do not look forward to what may happen tomorrow, the same everlasting Father who cares for you today will take care of you tomorrow and every day. He will either shield you from suffering, or He will give you unfailing strength to bear it."[4]

Secondly, remember our faith is strengthened through suffering by looking for God's Provision.

1 Thessalonians 5:18 – *Give thanks in all circumstances; for this is God's will for you in Christ Jesus. (NIV)*

This verse doesn't say we have to give thanks FOR the trial, but IN the trial. Fixing our eyes on how God has provided, even in the smallest ways, changes our focus from our circumstances and turns it towards Him. I remember being thankful that we didn't have to pay for hospital parking when our son was a patient for sixty-four days. It was just one of the ways God was providing for us.

Gratitude also creates perspective. It helps us to step outside of our situation and look at it from another's point of view. I was privileged to read the life stories of Corrie Ten Boom, Jim Elliott, and Gladys Alward. What they and their families endured makes my trials look like pittance. Their stories give me courage. They praised God—even for their suffering—because they wouldn't have become who they were without the struggles.

The third principle that has helped us is to remember God's faithfulness in the past, including the mountaintops. Why are we so quick to blame God for the low points of our sine curve, but not praise Him for the bountiful blessings? About six years ago, one of my worst nightmares came true. Toby had a four to six-hour convulsive seizure that left doctors scratching their heads. Most of the medicines aimed to stop the seizure weren't working. Towards the end, his body was so worn that his little body could only tremble. I wasn't sure he would ever wake up. I didn't know if he would ever again wrap his little arms around my neck to tell me he loved me.

I was angry and sure that God had somehow missed this one. All the other events in our lives had been lovingly sifted through His hands, but not this one. Sometimes, I'd think that because our family had been through so much that we should automatically get a free pass on future suffering. One of my favorite quotes is from a fictional book by Jan Karon. In it, the main character is struggling with this very issue and says, "I'm ashamed to confess it, but I thought I knew my true worth to God, I thought my faithfulness had long ago been revealed to Him. I didn't think He'd require anything more."[5]

When this situation came to us, a friend gently reminded me that God wasn't looking the other way. He knew it was coming and was with us. He was going to be our strength and our shield, our ever-present help in time of need (Psalm 18:2). And she was right. He never left us. He was there the whole time—sustaining, comforting, and loving. He provided family to care for our other three children, meals from strangers, and support from Lifepoint, a new church we'd just started attending about four weeks before this event. Honestly, I didn't know complete strangers could be so kind. I learned to trust by looking back over the past several years and remembering how He had provided in the past. When the children of Israel crossed the Jordan River led by Joshua, God instructed them to collect stones as they went and build an altar on the other side. This "altar" was a way to remember God's faithfulness and His provision.

I can't say for sure why God chose this very difficult path for us. I will admit with thankfulness that we wouldn't know Him in the way we do if not for Toby's illness. I know my own sinful heart. And if I'm honest, I see pride, independence, and a need to be in control. God has used this situation repeatedly to draw me back to Him. He has taught me greater trust and deeper compassion for others, while he gently reminds me that His plan is much greater than my own. He sees the front of the tapestry, while I only see the individual colors and threads. He's using Toby to reach others for His kingdom, and that's worth it.

It's not easy to see our son hurt, and his pain is not always physical…it's emotional too. But God has given Toby a joy that lights up a room. His smile is contagious, and when he faces a new trial, he will say, "I've faced thirty-nine surgeries; of course I can do this!" He knows he can do hard things because he's done them before through God's strength. Without God, we couldn't face these valleys, but praise be to God that He IS with us.

Psalm 41:1-2 – *I waited patiently for the LORD; he turned to me and heard my cry. He lifted me out of the slimy pit, out of the mud and mire; he set my feet on a rock and gave me a firm place to stand. He put a new song in my mouth, a hymn of praise to our God. Many will see and fear the LORD and put their trust in him. (NIV)*

A Next Step:

In our suffering it can be difficult, to say the least, to be grateful. Take a moment to think about how God has provided for you even during life's most challenging seasons. What did He teach you during those times? How did He draw close to you in the midst of your pain? Pray and thank God that He never leaves us nor forsakes us, especially in our pain.

_____

_____

_____

_____

_____

_____

_____

_____

_____

_____

_____

_____

_____

_____

_____

_____

_____

_____

_____

_____

_____

_____

_____

_____

_____

DAY 23

ASKING GOSPEL QUESTIONS

How Questions Can Create Patterns in Our Lives

– Adam P.

I love questions. They are powerful. Questions remind us that we don't know everything. Questions also remind others that they are worth our time because we value their thoughts and beliefs. So, I have a question for you:

When you think back to the best day of your life, what comes to mind?

I don't know about you, but I can't choose just one day as the best day of my life. I've had some great days. And, almost always, my great days have included great news. For instance, when Molly said, "Yes!" (and then, "I do!"). Or when the doctor said it was a healthy baby boy…and then a girl…and another girl…and another boy! Still, more important and life transforming than any of those days is the one where I discovered the good news that is the BEST news—the Gospel of Jesus Christ.

Gospel literally means good news. And the good news isn't about us. It's about Jesus. That's actually something you might find helpful to remind yourself from time to time…it's not about me; it's about Him. The Gospel is the good news that God, the Father, sent God, the Son, in the power of God, the Spirit, to conquer sin and death. Jesus accomplished this by His perfect life, His excruciating death on the cross, and His resurrection. Jesus is now seated at the right hand of God the Father and is the King of Heaven and Earth. He invites everybody everywhere to trust Him, to repent of our sin, and to seek to obey Him in everything we do. We do this acknowledging that it is only by grace that we've been saved. We don't save ourselves; God saves us.

The Gospel is bursting with implications for our lives. The Gospel reminds us that we are undeniably flawed, but unbelievably loved. It reminds us that every person we've ever met is a sinner. Your parents are sinners. Your siblings are sinners. Your friends are sinners. Your spouse is a sinner. Your kids are sinners. You are sinner. And what do sinners do? You guessed it! They sin! And sin hurts people. Sometimes we sin on accident…sometimes on purpose. The Gospel message reminds us of two critical insights for all of our relationships:

1. People are sinners. We will need to give them grace and seek to help them grow.
2. We are sinners. We will need to humbly receive grace and help to grow.

Further, the Gospel doesn't merely remind us of these insights. The Gospel gives us both the pattern and the power to give and receive grace. In Christ, we already know what it looks like to forgive others. In fact, we know what it looks like to give everything you have —even your very life—to forgive those you love. Jesus is our pattern for how to live life. But Jesus isn't just the One we look to for how to live. He's also the One who gives us the Holy Spirit. Romans 5 tells us, "God's love has been poured into our hearts through the Holy Spirit who has been given to us." The Holy Spirit empowers us to receive and to give God's love—a supernatural, life-changing kind of love. In Jesus, we see the example for healthy relationships, and we receive the power we need to cultivate those relationships.

Knowing that, how can we help one another grow in our conformity to the pattern of Jesus' life and death? How can we grow in our experience of His power at work in our lives? I believe that part of the answer is through regular, intentional conversations—especially with those closest to us. Through Gospel-centered conversations, we honor what the writer of Hebrews encourages believers to do:

Hebrews 10:24-25 – *And let us consider how to stir up one another to love and good works, not neglecting to meet together, as in the habit of some, but encouraging*

*one another, and all the more as you see the Day draw-
ing near.*

Now, I have an assignment for you. Obviously, I
can't make you do anything...but if you're interested
in helping yourself and others more fully experience
the pattern and power of the Gospel in your lives,
then I think you'll find these conversations incredibly powerful...eventually. To be honest, I think
you should know that you'll probably find them
to be a bit awkward at first. That's okay. Awkward
conversations can change lives.

So, here's your assignment: I'd like you to think
of two people who are very important to you. For
one of these people, I'd recommend including your
significant other, if you're married or in a romantic
relationship. Once you've chosen your two, schedule
a time to meet with them and discuss your answers
to the questions below. Ask all four questions (and
actively listen while they speak), and then they'll
ask you. And later you should do it again. (If you're
like me, you'll find this incredibly life-giving, and
you'll do it again and again and again...but that's
up to you.)

Conversations that point our attention towards
Jesus:

1. How are you doing? (Pro Tip: You can ask
    this same question by dividing it into two
    more specific questions. You can ask, "What
    are a couple of things that are going really
    well right now?" And then, "What are a cou-
    ple of things that you wish were going better

right now?" Using the exact words isn't what's important. What's important is finding a way to ask people how they are really doing... and then listen.)

2. What is God saying to you? (Pro Tip: Sometimes people forget that the Spirit of God uses the Word of God to speak to us. People might make up some pretty off the wall stuff. In response, you can help guard them from that by asking, "What Scripture is relevant to that?")

3. What are you going to do about that? (Pro Tip: Sometimes it's appropriate to ask for specifics. For example, if I tell you I'm "going to pray more," then you should know that I probably have no idea how I'm going to actually do that. So, you can lovingly ask things like: "What does 'praying more' look like for you? When do you think will be the best time during the day to add this prayer time? When are you going to begin this new habit?")

4. How can I pray for you? (Pro Tip: Never underestimate how beautiful and powerful it is to simply pray out loud for someone else. The prayer of a righteous person has great power as it is working!)

I hope you take me up on this little assignment and learn the power of questions to help others. But more than any of that, I hope you experience the joy and power of Jesus in your life...and remember that, in Him, your best days are yet to come.

Day 23 Key Concept: Start intentional, Gospel-centered conversations

A Next Step:

Take the time to follow this chapter's assignment. Before you begin, pray that God would give you the diligence and desire to complete the task. Also, pray for the others you'll ask to join you, that they would be open to growing in deeper relationship with God and others.

_____

_____

_____

_____

_____

_____

_____

_____

_____

_____

_____

_____

_____

_____

DAY 24
BLENDED FAMILIES

Navigating the New Normal

– Kevin & Carrie H.

While I was dating my wife, Carrie, I was trying to make a good impression with her daughter, Sarah, who was five years old at the time. Sarah loved to sit on my shoulders, and I would run around Carrie's condo pretending to be an airplane. On one particular night, Carrie was experiencing the typical parent-child struggle at bedtime. In other words, Carrie wanted Sarah in bed, but Sarah wasn't cooperating. This bedtime battle between Carrie and Sarah was common and had a tendency to escalate to epic proportions. Becoming acutely familiar with this struggle and foreseeing where the negotiations were headed, I decided to defuse the situation. Not only that, I figured I could strengthen my relationship with Sarah by showing her how fun I could be at bedtime, while impressing Carrie with my seasoned parenting skills. After all, I had a daughter of my own who was ten, and I knew a thing or two about single parenthood.

Thinking that Sarah just needed to expend a little extra energy before she settling down for the night, I asked her if she wanted to go for a ride on my shoulders. Her resistance to going to bed quickly transitioned to excitement as she ran to me with open arms. I put her on my shoulders and pretended to be an airplane flying around Carrie's condo. But this time, I decided to try something a little different. I began acting like I was about to crash and would quickly turn away to miss obstacles throughout the room. Sarah loved it! She was laughing so hard that she could hardly breathe. Then it happened…I began to feel something warm against the back of my neck and this sensation started running down my back. Much to my surprise, she was laughing "out of control."

I quickly took Sarah off my shoulders, and she ran with excitement to Carrie giggling, "That was so much fun Mommy. I want to do that again!" I maintained an awkward smile as I discreetly informed Carrie what had happened. Needless to say, our date night was cut short. I had to make a quick exit for much needed clean up, and I left Carrie with a five-year-old who was even more wound up than before. Not to mention, Sarah now needed a little cleaning of her own. While I may have achieved a new level of closeness with Sarah, I failed miserably trying to impress Carrie with my well-honed parenting skills.

Now that Carrie and I have been married for six years and Sarah is almost a teenager, our whole family still laughs about that night. However, there's a hidden truth in this story. Blending families can be messy, and they take a lot of time to cultivate. Still, the reward that comes from building a healthy blended family far outweighs the hard work that is required to make it work.

Carrie has two daughters, Chloe and Sarah, who are fourteen and twelve. I have one daughter, Meredith, who is seventeen. In addition to being married for six years, Carrie and I dated two years before getting married. Even with all of this time together, we are still learning about stepfamily dynamics and how to blend two families together. One thing we've learned is that cultivating healthy relationships and creating a home environment that is stable, secure, and dependable cannot occur overnight and cannot be forced.

In the majority of cases, it's the parents who are the most interested in making a blended family "work." This stands to reason because it is the parents who came together in marriage and brought everyone under one roof. In their sincere effort of trying to create strong relationships and a healthy home environment, one or both of the parents often begins to force the issue, which is where problems begin.

Children, whether they are minors or adults, are typically less interested and even resistant to the thought of becoming part of a blended family. From their perspective, they are being forced into a family dynamic in which they had very little or no input. Most people who are forced into something take one of two approaches: 1) they demonstrate compliance without any desire of wanting more or 2) they rebel against what they are being forced to do. So, it should come as no surprise that children of blended families are not as excited as their parents about the new family and may resist the thought of a new blended family.

In many cases, children haven't completed the grieving process from the loss of their prior family, whether caused from the death of a parent or divorce. Hence, they will likely be even more resistant to the thought of participating in a new blended family environment. Add to this the complexity of potentially multiple marriages from the parent(s), and one can quickly see why the child of a blended family might be hesitant to build new relationships or be resistant to the new home environment.

Parents who force the issue of making sure all parties within the family get along tend to experience increased tension, instability, and resistance from their children. At times, a better option for parents could be providing space to allow their children to move at their own unique pace. A healthy relationship can only grow as fast as the one who moves the slowest. The one who desires the relationship to move faster must exhibit patience and grace. Here is probably one of the hardest things to accept in any relationship but particularly difficult in a blended family: the person who desires a closer relationship must accept the fact that the relationship may never be as close as he or she wants it to be.

When we think about how Jesus pursues us, He gives us the freedom to choose how closely we want to follow Him. Jesus doesn't coerce, convince, or contrive people to be in relationship with Him. He doesn't force us to love Him, read our Bibles or go to church, because true love cannot be forced. Instead, Jesus' love for us is patient and kind, and His love sets the standard for how we are to love others:

Ephesians 4:1-2 – *walk in a manner worthy of the calling to which you have been called, with all humility and gentleness, with patience, bearing one another in love.*

To the extent that parents of blended families can express Christ's love in the way He's shown to us, they will enable their children to move at their own unique pace and begin to grow closer in a blended family environment.

Day 24 Key Concept: A healthy relationship can only grow as fast as the one who moves the slowest.

A Next Step:

At times, we have relationships that feel more distant than we'd like, and that distance can sometimes lead to feelings of rejection or bitterness. Take some time today and pray for those distant relationships in your life. Pray that God would give you patience, grace, and love towards the other person and that He would help grow you closer together.

_____

_____

_____

_____

_____

_____

_____

_____

_____

_____

_____

_____

_____

_____

_____

_____

_____

_____

_____

_____

_____

_____

_____

_____

_____

_____

_____

DAY 25
ADOPTION

A Tragically Beautiful Gift
– Matt & Kristy L.

From the time we were married, we agreed to be open to growing our family through adoption should the Lord move us in that direction. Many years later, it wasn't a surprise to either of us when we sensed that it was time. We knew it would be challenging and that there was a lot we didn't understand, but we held onto the promise that the Lord would give us strength. What we soon discovered is that NOTHING could have prepared us for how God would use the pain and joy of adopting our son to reveal the depth of our own orphanhood and adoption into His family.

Romans 8:15-17 – For you did not receive the spirit of slavery to fall back into fear, but you have received the Spirit of adoption as sons, by whom we cry "Abba Father!" The Spirit himself bears witness with our spirit that we are the children of God, and if children, then heirs—heirs of God and fellow heirs with Christ, provided we suffer with him in order that we may also be glorified with him.

We remember being so excited to bring our son home. As any expectant parent, there was so much anticipation and hope. Our older son couldn't wait to meet his brother. Call us naive, but somehow (even after reading plenty of material telling us otherwise) we honestly thought that our deep love for this child would miraculously and immediately be felt and received by him…at least to some degree.

Spoiler alert: that's not exactly how this story goes. With adoption, there is great loss to be mourned and a cost to be counted.

Trauma, loss, grief, attachment. These are words that those familiar with the reality of adoption are often well acquainted. Most would agree that the effects of trauma and loss on a child can range from subtle and sneaky to blatant and debilitating. Our son's story is his to tell, but we can openly and confidently say that adoption doesn't take place without the cost of great loss being paid. The moments, days, weeks, months and years that followed were some of the most challenging of our lives.

The real story went like this:

Parents (and brother): Give love, compassion, patience, kindness, and gentleness (albeit imperfectly).

Child: Responds frantically with screaming, avoidance, hitting, running, fear, confusion, mistrust, and withdrawal.

Repeat.

Parents (and brother): Through tears, TRY to be loving, compassionate, patient, kind, and gentle.

Child: Responds with a fleeting moment of trust, a hug, a smile, and the softening of his heart towards us. Then immediately repeats first response.

Repeat entire cycle 10,000 more times. Come close, get away, come close, get away, come close, get away.

The truth is that for so long, the grief of loss and the fear of future abandonment and rejection were far more REAL to our sweet son's heart than the truth of our love, which was fully available to him from day one.

And there, in the midst of the pain and struggle, was the slow awakening to the condition of our own hearts.

Day 25 Key Concept: Adoption mirrors our story

In Christ, we have full access to what our hearts so desperately desire. We have access to the patient, kind, gentle, faithful, unconditional love of Abba Father. Yet, so often, our own loss and trauma follows us into our relationship with Him.

We so desperately crave and long for the safe harbor and refuge of the Father's love, but shame spurs us to hide and withdraw. The fear of abandonment or rejection is the impetus to our scoffing at His love for us. As a result, we find ourselves as the scared child, caught in an unending cycle of push-pull with the Lord. "Come close, get away, come close, get away."

He knows you've been wounded. He knows you have lost and grieved much. He knows you've been rejected and abandoned. He knows you are scared. Yet, His reply is, "Fear not." His love is more patient and kind and gentle and faithful than anything you have experienced in this broken world.

John 4:18 – *There is no fear in love, but perfect love casts out fear...*

And your adoption also came at the cost of great loss.

Jesus is no stranger to abandonment, rejection, and loss. Judas, one of his own disciples, betrayed him for money. Peter, his close friend, denied their relationship three times and then abandoned Him during His last hours. The very people He loved and came for rejected Him, nailing Him to a tree. And there on the cross, the ultimate cost was paid. God the Father removed His presence from His beloved Son and poured out His wrath upon Him, the wrath that you and I deserved. In that moment, Jesus suffered the loss and abandonment of His Father, so that those who call upon His name would no longer be slaves to fear. And as Christ is resurrected, so are we. Sealed by the Holy Spirit, we see His promise fulfilled.

John 14:18-19 – *I will not leave you as orphans; I will come to you. In a little while, the world will see Me no more, but you will see Me. Because I live, you also will live.*

Adoption is one of the most tragically beautiful gifts given to us. Adoption reflects the heart of God the Father. He reconciles the lost, the broken, the hopeless, the afraid, the abandoned and the rejected unto Himself. Not as slaves to fear, but as His children, perfectly loved and safe in the arms of our Father.

Today, our family looks much different than in those early days. By God's grace, we didn't give up on each other. In His grace, how much more will our Heavenly Father not give up on us!

A Next Step:

Adoption is a beautiful reflection of what God has done for us. Take some time to pray for the orphans of the world. Pray that God would give them loving homes to live in and that they would know and follow Jesus Christ. Maybe take the time to encourage someone you know who has adopted a child and pray for their family.

_____

_____

_____

_____

_____

_____

_____

_____

_____

_____

_____

_____

_____

_____

_____

_____

_____

_____

_____

_____

_____

_____

_____

_____

_____

_____

_____

_____

_____

_____

_____

_____

_____

DAY 26
MARRIAGE & MINISTRY

Opposites Attract

– Ed T.

Have you ever noticed that opposites attract? Most of the time? This couldn't be truer of my wife and me. Tammy and I have been married for twenty-plus years, and it still amazes me how differently we see the world. I'm the youngest of six kids…she's an only child. I'm an extrovert…she's an introvert. She likes clutter…I like order. She wants to fall asleep with the TV on…I want all the lights off. And those are just the parts of the iceberg that you can see! Sometimes our differences cause conflict, and we're forced to work to understand each other. After two decades of marriage, I can say that opposites really do attract.

The Bible has much to say about marriage, and one place to look is The Book of Proverbs:

Proverbs 18:22 – *He who finds a wife finds a good thing and obtains favor from the LORD.*

Clearly, God must have a reason for taking Tammy and me, two people with such different personalities, and bringing us together in marriage. In fact, God is doing me a favor! I bring this up because I believe God wants all marriages to reflect His Glory to others. We should always be ready to give a reason for the hope that He has put inside of us (1 Pet. 3:15), and marriage gives us the opportunity to work together in that way. One way I get to see God working our differences out for His Glory is in the area of evangelism. Let me share an example of how this works in our marriage.

For the last fifteen years, I've been working as a pastor, and for three years before that I led a collegiate ministry. When I led that collegiate Bible study of about fifteen people, we decided to have a Super Bowl party. Our intention was to have everyone invite friends, so we could connect with others who weren't part of our group. I was very excited when the party started because we had at least thirty people show up. About an hour into the party, Tammy and I ran into two girls who had been occasionally attending our Bible study. Christina was from Brazil, and Jeanette was from Costa Rica. They were working as au pairs and had recently become friends. In conversation, it became clear that Christina was a follower of Jesus, while Jeanette had yet to make that decision. I asked Jeanette if she understood the Gospel, and she said that she didn't but wanted to know more.

This is where Tammy and I work really well together. Sharing the Gospel has always been a passion of mine. Answering questions about the Bible, science, other religions or just skeptical questions is something that I actually get excited about. Now, Tammy is all heart! She has a very unique way of understanding people, and she easily relates the Gospel to their hearts in a way that I struggle to do. She is very patient while I answer questions, but there are times when she can just take over a conversation and help people know Jesus.

Back to the story. There we were, sitting behind a couch at the host home of this Super Bowl party. The four of us sat in a circle and were about to engage in a life-changing conversation while a couple dozen college-aged students cheered for their favorite team. I asked Jeanette what she believed about Jesus. Here's the summary of her belief—she needs to do enough good to outweigh the bad she's done to get into Heaven. I explained that if her ideas were true, if it's about our actions, then Jesus never would've had to die on the Cross. I shared with her God's grace and mercy as demonstrated on the Cross and how we can never do enough good to make up for our bad behavior. The reason is simple—God is perfect. If He were to just let us in, then we would bring all of our imperfections into His perfect Heaven. Our holy God cannot tolerate sin, so something had to be done. Jesus shed His blood to wash away all of our sins, and He wants to become the Lord of our lives. Then, I asked Jeanette if she believed this and wanted Jesus to become her Lord and Savior.

During the conversation, Christina and Tammy didn't say much. They chimed in a bit about their experiences, but they were mostly patiently listening. Jeanette did want Jesus to become her Lord and Savior, so the four of us held hands and prayed. I led us in prayer but prompted Jeanette to pray as well, even in her native language if it felt more comfortable. I'd pray and then prompt her. She'd pray in Portuguese, and then it was back to me. This happened for a while, until I prompted Jeanette to ask for God's forgiveness. But nothing happened. She fell silent. To be honest, I had no idea what to do, so…I waited. Suddenly, it felt as if someone was dripping water on my hand. I looked up to see Jeanette crying. When asked what was wrong, she said she'd done too much wrong, just too much and looked pained with guilt.

I froze and had no idea what to do. Tammy, who had been patiently praying, let go of our hands and grabbed Jeanette's. She looked into her eyes and said, "He wants to forgive you. You just need to ask Him." Those words helped Jeanette start praying again, and afterwards I thanked the Lord for what He was doing and going to do in her life. After I said "Amen," Jeanette and Christina hugged and cried together. I looked over at Tammy, and all I could think about was how grateful I was that she was my wife. She seemed to know exactly what was going on in Jeanette's heart and how to speak to her in that moment.

Genesis 2:18 – *Then the Lord God said, "It is not good that man should be alone; I will make a helper fit for him."*

Oh, how true this is! Our marriages should reflect the Glory of God and point others to Him. God uses both husbands and wives to do this very thing. When it comes to sharing the Gospel with others, God gives us exactly the spouse we need to accomplish this purpose together. A perfect compliment!

Day 26 Key Concept: Let your marriage be an instrument for His purposes

As a pastor, I hear couples make many complaints about each other. Often couples will struggle because of their differences. I want to encourage you to see that God uses our differences for His purposes in our lives. If we take the time to understand why we see things differently, it will often lead to resolution. Remember that God uses the differences in our marriage to sanctify and grow us. Some people think that God will never be able to use their marriage to make a Gospel-difference in the world. That process begins with offering your life and marriage to be a tool for His purposes. Start to pray about this together. As you pray that God uses your life and marriage for His purposes, keep watch for how God puts you in situations to point others to Himself! It may be a simple as inviting someone to church or a small group. It might be asking someone about his or her faith journey. Just offer your life and marriage to the Lord in prayer together and just watch what He does!

A Next Step:

Evangelism can sometimes feel scary. We wonder if we'll say the wrong thing or scare off others, leaving them thinking we are nuts! However, as Christians, we are called to share the good news of Jesus Christ. Pray that God would put people in your path with whom you can share the Gospel. Pray that He would give you the words to say and the courage to share your faith.

_____

_____

_____

_____

_____

_____

_____

_____

_____

_____

_____

_____

_____

DAY 27
A PEACEFUL HOUSE

How to Fight Fair

– Steve & Lisa C.

"Put on then, as God's chosen ones, holy and beloved, compassionate hearts, kindness, humility, meekness, and patience, bearing with one another and, if one has a complaint against another, forgiving each others; as the Lord has forgiven you, so you must also forgive. And above all these put on love, which binds everything together in perfect harmony. And let the peace of Christ rule in your hearts, to which indeed you were called in one body. And be thankful." Colossians 3:12-15

My husband and I have been married for a little over three years, and it's been crazy! It's a second marriage for both of us, so we have a blended family with five children spanning ages two to eighteen.

We have teenagers, preteens, and toddlers. I repeat—teenagers, preteens, and toddlers! We like to say we put the "fun" in dysfunctional. Steve is an entrepreneur and is constantly dreaming up ideas for businesses and products; he never stops. I like to joke that he is my version of Edward Cullen, the vampire from Twilight, while I am an average human who needs to sleep and occasionally sit down and watch TV.

Building a new marriage, blending two families together, and attempting to co-parent with ex-spouses come with A LOT of conflict. Throughout the process, the Lord continues to teach us (and humble us) how to manage contention in our lives. There are days when we fail—sometimes miserably—but we continue to try. We know that conflict comes in all forms and is in every part of our lives. So, whether the battle is within ourselves, with outside influences, or with each other, our goal is always peace and redemption.

Day 27 Key Concept: Pursue peace at any cost

The Conflict Within:

To overcome conflict, we need to be at peace with God and within ourselves. It all starts there. The above verses from Colossians say, "Let the peace of Christ rule in your hearts." We all experience inner challenges that prevent us from being our best, so we have to get ourselves right before we can make any other situation right.

I am a worrier and an over-thinker. I have always struggled with this, and at times, my worries and fears have been paralyzing—especially during conflict. My husband is the opposite and acts before thinking things through to the end. Then, if needed, he corrects himself, all the while NOT WORRYING. It's amazing to me. No matter how we work through conflict, I think we all wonder if we are doing the right things. Are we doing what God wants us to do? Are we doing enough? What I've learned is that even if we do our best, it will never be enough. But we don't have to worry! We will fail and make mistakes because we're not—and never will be—perfect. Our Savior, Jesus Christ, is perfect, and He has a perfect love for us.

Action Step: Check yourself.

When conflict arises, check yourself first. We all communicate and experience life differently. Are we being defensive? Are we communicating effectively? How may have we contributed to the conflict? Do we care more about being right than about resolution? Be honest and get to a place of humility. What can we learn from this? What is God trying to teach us? Embrace humility. It starts with us.

The External Challenges:

Life happens, and we take the good with the bad. Sometimes it happens all at once. In the last five years, we've dealt with our share of "life." A business failing, moving three times, extreme hearing loss, the birth of our fifth child who was unplanned, a family member's drug addiction, the unexpected full custody of three of our kids, two new jobs, living apart across the country, and our teenager's near fatal car accident...just to name a few. In these moments, we've been humbled down to nothing and have learned the toughest lessons. At the same time, they are the moments we've felt the most loved by God.

The majority of us spend more time working than on any other part of our lives. Financial stability is something we all strive for, and often times we prioritize money over many eternal aspects of our lives. Steve's experienced highs and lows in personal business, and as a result, highs and lows in financial stability. At some points, he felt in control, and other times he realized he had no control over the outcomes. Recently, Steve founded a company, and it became the shining star of both the mainstream media and the investment community. Being on top was easy and fun! Now contrast that with having to let every employee of that same company go when he had to shut it down. It was brutal, painful, and beyond humbling. The most important lesson he learned was that no matter whether he was being interviewed on The Opening Bell on Fox News or hiding under a table in shame, God didn't care. Steve had to be humble enough to let God grow him in the ways that He wanted. This external conflict was uncontrollable; however, there was one thing he could control—his attitude. He was blessed with another day and another opportunity to be thankful, to smile, and to keep enjoying every opportunity God creates.

Action Step: Control the Controllables.

There is much peace that comes when we recognize that we're not in control, but God is. This is one lesson some of us keep having to learn. And re-learn. When we surrender ourselves to God, our burden is lifted, and we can continue on the path the Lord has planned for us. He is in control, and His way will bring us to joy and peace.

Harmony in Marriage:

Statistics for marriages are pretty grim. Statistics for second blended marriages are even worse. We HAVE to keep our marriages strong to survive all that life throws at us.

Because my husband and I are very different, at times it's been difficult for us to resolve conflict. We've discovered that we need to be in the right mindset to have any discussion regarding conflict. Only then can we truly understand each other's perspectives and appreciate our differences. Once there is true understanding, there is always resolution and healing.

Action Step: Validation, Accountability and Forgiveness.

To truly understand each other, we need to validate each other's experiences and perspectives. Conflict does damage—especially when not resolved.

Wounds will not heal without a sincere apology and change of behavior. We need to own our actions or words that have hurt others and then forgive each other. Forgiveness is the last step and is often the hardest. However, we've been promised that when we do these things, our lives, marriages, and families will be blessed.

Conflict is unavoidable. It's part of our daily lives, and we are required to overcome it as followers of Christ. As we strive to become more like Him, we will develop all the tools necessary to find inner peace in reliance upon Jesus and within our marriages or relationships. "And let the peace of Christ rule in your hearts."

A Next Step:

We live in world that encourages us to vent and get everything off our chests. Plus, there's the fact that the world of social media is littered with mean comments and put-downs. As a result, it can be easy to think we have the right to say whatever we please to whomever we please. Take some time to remember that our God is the God of peace. Pray that He would help you to live peaceably with others and to resolve the conflict in your midst as much as it is possible.

_____

_____

_____

_____

_____

_____

_____

_____

_____

_____

_____

_____

_____

_____

_____

_____

_____

_____

_____

_____

_____

_____

_____

_____

_____

_____

_____

_____

_____

_____

_____

_____

DAY 28

ONCE A MAN, TWICE A CHILD

Caring for Aging Parents
– John & Jenifer W.

Do you remember the wisdom from that great theologian Forrest Gump? "Life was like a box of chocolates. You never know what you're gonna get." But when I was a kid, I liked the Whitman Chocolate Sampler that Dad bought Mom every Valentine's Day because you knew what you were getting. That way, you didn't end up with the mallow cream instead of caramel.

As much as we like to think that life is like a Whitman's chocolate, we know better. We do not get to choose our life's experiences or challenges.

My father passed away in 1995 from cancer, and my mom lived in the home they shared, until it

became obvious that she needed help. We moved
Mom into a condo close to my wife and me for a
few years, until it became clear that she needed
even more care. So, Mom moved in with us. A short
time later, Mom was diagnosed with Alzheimer's
disease. Over the course of the next ten years, my
wife Jenifer and I cared for Mom, first in our home
and later in a nursing home.

In our experience, those afflicted with Alzheimer's
regress one step at a time. The individual is at one
level for a while, and then there is a noticeable
drop in cognition. At first the memory lapses can
be humorous. While Mom was living with us, our
son was playing college baseball in Kentucky, so on
Saturday's in the fall we would drive to Kentucky
to watch him play. We would always take Mom
with us because she couldn't be left alone, and all
the way Mom would repeatedly ask if I was "taking
her to a home."

With that history you can imagine how difficult
it was to actually take Mom to live in an assisted
living memory unit. The anxiety and guilt were
overwhelming. The inevitable question of whether
you are doing it for yourself or for her just nags
at your soul. You don't want to be selfish, but the
care needed becomes more than most families can
provide.

As her disease progressed, Mom slowly lost
the part of her that made her unique, and for the
last few years she no longer recognized her family.
Jenifer and I would go to the nursing home three
or four times a week. I would sit by Mom and hold
her hand. Occasionally people asked why I would

continue to go week after week after week, when Mom no longer recognized me. My response was always the same—because I know who she is. She is the woman who sat at the breakfast table when I was in elementary school and prayed and read the Bible to me. Mom had done what any godly parent is charged to do—she passed on her faith to her children.

Mom passed away in 2015. A few months after Mom died, we learned that Jenifer's mother had Dementia. In some respects, it is more difficult the second time around because you know what is coming, and we try to remind ourselves that today is the best day she will ever have.

To add to the situation, Jenifer's father is 85-years-old and trying to care for her mother at home. All the while, he is making himself ill trying to do so. He needs someone to care for him, yet he is trying to care for his wife. At times, he lashes out at the ones who love him the most because of his own anger and frustration over his wife of sixty-two years' condition. We understand his emotions, but it's still hard to bear the brunt of his frustration.

Jenifer receives calls from her brother or the home healthcare worker telling her that her father has fallen or become ill and has been taken to the hospital. As a result, Jenifer has to rush two hours away and take care of her mother for weeks at times. This is the season of life Jenifer is in now. Even though it's difficult, she is thankful that God has made it possible for her to be available to her parents.

Even from our home, Jenifer calls her parents every day. She "talks" to her mother, even though it can hardly be called a conversation. Still, every conversation ends with, "I love you, Mom." Even though Jenifer's mom needs to be in a nursing home, her father still insists on caring for her at their home. While everyone gives you advice on what should be done, forcing her father to do something he doesn't want to do is virtually impossible.

We provide care to our parents the best we know how and endure the frustrations along with the well-intentioned (but often painful) "advice/criticism" offered by others. And we remember what God's word has to say:

Galatians 6:9 – *And let us not grow weary of doing good, for in due season we will reap, if we do not give up.*

We have seen reaping in the midst of such hardship. For instance, Jenifer's mother has collected Precious Moments figurines for years, and she has hundreds displayed around her home. Sometimes, during Jenifer's trips to her mom's home, her mom will grasp her hand or seemingly out of the blue tell Jen that she loves her. Jenifer feels those are the real precious moments that God gives to her. Those moments remind her that, even through the cloud of Dementia, her mom is still there, and that Jen's expressions of love and kindness are appreciated.

Scripture also reveals that we are to, "Honor your father and mother." When we were young, we used to think that meant taking their advice, being a good student, and not getting into trouble. At this stage of life, it takes on a whole different meaning.

Even more, God's word tells us to love each other and delight in honoring others:

Romans 12:10 – *Love each other with genuine affection, and take delight in honoring each other. (NLT)*

For me, caring for my mother for a decade was not what I considered a burden. I was the youngest of four children and the only boy. My sisters would tell you that I lived a "charmed life," and that "it was never much of a secret who was Mom and Dad's favorite." To some extent, that is true; however, the real reason I cared for Mom was because of the love of Christ she instilled in me. Yes, there was a lot of sacrifice involved, but all of that paled in comparison to the debt that I owed by parents for leading me to faith in Jesus.

I don't know of any magical formula for how to navigate the tough terrain when your father and mother no longer have the ability to care for themselves. What I do know is that love conquers all. And not just the love between a parent and a child, but the kind of love that comes from a relationship with the One who is love.

Day 28 Key Concept: Let the love of Christ fuel your love towards others

Caring for aging parents is a one-day-at-a-time kind of thing, especially with Dementia because of the inevitable descent, so enjoy today. Spend as much time as you can with your loved ones, because you don't want to experience the pain of regret. Also, remember how your parents cared for you and the sacrifices they made on your behalf. That, in itself, will provide motivation, when you compare what they gave to you with the few years you may need to give back to them.

In addition, think about those special times in your life when you felt your parent(s) earned the title "Best Mom or Dad in the World." In such times, you felt loved, safe, and important. We don't often know exactly what our elderly parents are thinking. However, I think it's safe to say that they long to feel loved, safe, and important. Finally, enjoy the "Precious Moments" while you can, and be thankful God has given you this time to return the love your parents so abundantly poured out on you.

A Next Step:

Our parents have sacrificed so much for us, and often times, we don't thank them enough. Reach out to your parent(s) and thank them for all they've done for you. Perhaps you could send them a card with a quick note letting them know you've seen their sacrifice and are grateful for it. If your parents are no longer with you, then thank God for giving you your parents and for all of the ways He cares for you, as your Heavenly Father.

DAY 29

MARRIAGE & MISSION

Loving Each Other to Love the World

– Brian & Heidi F.

Every marriage is different, and we recognize that not everyone begins marriage with God in the equation. We just happened to be Christians before we got married. However, even though we both were following Jesus, we didn't automatically understand how to connect our marriage with our mission. Sure, we made a covenant to love each other and be faithful to each other "until death do us part." But in the beginning, we didn't understand how much we would need to surrender our own selfish wants for the purpose of a thriving marriage, let alone a marriage on mission. Just like salvation, when we commit our whole selves to the Lord, life is not automatically without suffering. We sin. We rebel. We don't always know what to do. Yet, God redeems all those moments we surrender to Him.

Salvation is the first step to grow in our relationship with God. But trusting the Lord with our lives doesn't stop there. Something happens AFTER we trust Jesus as our Savior:

1 John 4:10-12 – *This is love: not that we loved God, but that He loved us and sent His Son as an atoning sacrifice for our sins. Dear friends, since God so loved us, we also ought to love one another. No one has ever seen God, but if we love one another, God lives in us and His love is made complete in us. (NIV)*

Sanctification—becoming more like Jesus—follows salvation. This is a lifelong process of growing in love and being conformed to the image of Christ. And while we're on that sanctification journey, marriage is an excellent teacher. Marriage is an opportunity to grow in love and to share God's love with others.

Our early years of marriage were challenging. We argued often and hard. For example, we would not only fight about who should take out the trash, but we'd also fight about who should replace the trash bag. We even argued about how we were arguing. We said mean words and gave each other the silent treatment. We fought to be heard and didn't always want to listen. We didn't want others to know how our marriage really felt sometimes. In those moments, we definitely were thinking about putting on a united "front" for others more than being on mission together to show God's love to others.

Still, amidst all the fumbling, we were trying to understand each other and learn how to make decisions together, while keeping God in our line of sight. It was our goal to honor God and love each other in our marriage, and we trusted that God would help us because His word says He will:

1 John 4:13-16 – *If anyone acknowledges that Jesus is the Son of God, God lives in them and they in God. And so we know and rely on the love God has for us. (NIV)*

With God's power, we learned to resolve our conflict more effectively. We had to ask God continually to lead us, when our natural inclination was to be mean and withhold forgiveness. In this process, we grew in our ability to trust each other and to love each other more deeply.

Pursuing each other after hurt, forgiving each other, and demonstrating unconditional love to each other was and is extremely hard work. But what happened over time is that we began shifting from "me" to "we," and we became a united team rather than a united front. We became a family who loved each other and who could effectively be on mission together to show others God's love.

Through the years, we've increased living on mission in our relationships with other people outside our family. We share meals with people. We share normal life with people. Sometimes it was as simple as letting children in our neighborhood see us loving each other and caring for them when they played with our boys. Sometimes it's leading couples through premarital counseling and sharing the mistakes and lessons we've learned along the way.

We have even stretched ourselves by inviting different people to live in our home for seasons. During those times, we learned a new depth of giving and receiving God's love in marriage and to others. Having someone outside our family live in our home, watching us parent our children, disagree with each other, serve each other, ignore each other, laugh together, offend each other, listen to, and forgive each other is a high level of accountability that we've chosen to expose ourselves to. But this is our marriage on mission. Running to each other with our hurts and embracing each other with grace and forgiveness is a tangible way to show others how to run to God. We trust that He will embrace us, His children, with unconditional love and forgiveness as well. As a family, our aim is to live out the words of John:

1 John 4:18-19 – *There is no fear in love. But perfect love drives out fear, because fear has to do with punishment. The one who fears is not made perfect in love. We love because He first loved us. (NIV)*

Imagine for a moment that your marriage was everything that you wanted it to be. If your marriage was full, exciting, rich, meaningful, and life giving how would it look? With that picture in mind, what would your marriage look like in practice?

1. What activities would you be doing regularly?
2. What benefits would you experience personally?
3. How would others be impacted by your marriage?

How would our marriages look if they were aligned around God's mission to bring healing and hope to the world through us? Maybe your mission needs to begin with working at loving your spouse with God's love. Maybe you need to decide together whom you need to invite into your home, so they can see you loving Jesus, loving each other, and also receiving love from you.

In the end, marriage and mission is simply:

1 John 4:16-17 – *God is love. Whoever lives in love lives in God, and God in them. This is how love is made complete among us so that we will have confidence on the Day of Judgment: In this world we are like Jesus. (NIV)*

Day 29 Key Concept: Our marriages should reflect God's mission

A Next Step:

Whether we are married or single, our lives, as Christians, are always on mission—to love others and point them to Jesus. What is your personal mission field? Who has God put into your life for you to reach? Can you reach people at work? In your neighborhood? In your family? Pray that God would help you live a life on mission.

_____
_____
_____
_____
_____
_____
_____
_____
_____
_____
_____
_____
_____
_____
_____
_____
_____
_____
_____
_____
_____
_____
_____
_____
_____
_____

DAY 30

WORK-LIFE BALANCE

How to Do the Most Important Things without
Burning Out

– Kary O.

Try balancing on one foot.

It's difficult, especially for any length of time.

Now try doing it while someone hands you car keys, a laptop, a coffee mug, running shoes, a bag of groceries, a basket of laundry, financial statements, cough medicine, a leaf blower, and just to top things off—a piece of cake. Remember, all while balancing on one foot.

In the words of Dr. Phil, "How is that working for you?"

This painful experience defines most people attempting to master work-life balance. But is this

what God intended for his children—constant striv-
ing and failing?

Consider the people of the Bible? Was the
Apostle Paul balanced in his missionary journeys?
Or Queen Esther in her attempt to rescue the nation
of Israel? What about Nehemiah building the wall?
Elijah running from Jezebel? Or even Jesus fulfilling
his 3-year ministry?

Although it might sound unpopular, none of
these people were balanced. Why? Because progress
requires unbalance. God tells us in His word we
were created for good works. Work means action
and action means unbalance.

Work ➜ Action ➜ Unbalance

Think about it.

Walking is controlled "falling." Every step we take
requires unbalance. The problem isn't getting unbalanced; it's staying unbalanced. Look around—the
price of staying unbalanced is quite costly. Headlines
of moral failure and burnout rip through our aware-
ness on a daily basis. Such people didn't just get
unbalanced; they stayed unbalanced.

Sure there's a fine line between getting unbalanced and staying unbalanced, but there's also a
secret to making it easier. The key is returning back
to our center of gravity on a regular basis. After a
sprint of unbalance, we need a place of rest and
recovery. We need a sacred space of clarity where
we get re-centered and refocused.

For me, this is my OPUS.

Maybe it's a new term to you—at least in this context. However, OPUS is the Latin word for work. It means masterpiece.

The other Latin word for work is LABOR, and it means toil. Every single person on planet earth is working. The real question is what type of work are we doing—LABOR or OPUS?

Work too long LABORING, and you'll burnout from unbalance. Work within your OPUS, and you'll experience rest and rejuvenation.

The Scriptures tell us we are God's masterpiece. In a sense, we are God's OPUS created to do good works.

Ephesians 2:10 – *For we are God's masterpiece. He has created us anew in Christ Jesus, so we can do the good things he planned for us long ago.* (NLT)

Let's get practical. What does it mean to get clear about your OPUS and do that OPUS on a daily basis? My friend Chet Scott of Built to Lead defines OPUS as:

O: Overarching Vision
P: Purpose
U: Unifying Strategies
S: Scorecard for Significance

Ask yourself. Do I have an over-arching vision, a clearly defined purpose, unifying strategies, and a scorecard for significance? If not, then you have no center of gravity. In the noise and distractions of life you'll be more likely to drift and stay unbalanced.

I know firsthand.

Years ago I was the poster child for unbalance. I had nothing to pull me back to center. Since I didn't want to be another statistic, I set out on a journey to discover my OPUS. In my book, The Deeper Path, I share that process. Today my OPUS helps me stay focused. (You can see an example of OPUS by reviewing mine at: KaryOberbrunner.com/OPUS)

Too many times we overcomplicate this whole work-life balance issue. This is the Enemy's strategy. While we debate the issue we stall out or burn out—settling for doing nothing OR doing everything.

Wisdom is doing a few things well. It's showing up, filled up with our entire heart, soul, mind, and strength. It's doing our OPUS every day. This is the definition of a "master" in the art of living:

> "Masters in the art of living draw no sharp distinction between their work and play, labor and leisure, mind and body, education and recreation. They hardly know which is which. They simply pursue their vision of excellence through whatever they're doing, and leave others to determine whether they're working or playing. To themselves, they always appear to be doing both."
> — L. P. Jacks

You have incredible valuable. God has given you tremendous talent, but it's your responsibility to steward those talents.

Jesus addressed this principle with a story in Matthew 25 about a faithful servant who took action and an unfaithful one who stayed put. The servant who pleased the master was the one who took action and got unbalanced—at least momentarily.

Matthew 25:23 – *His master said to him, "Well done, good and faithful servant. You have been faithful over a little; I will set you over much. Enter into the joy of your master."*

We have one of two choices. We can stay balanced and bury our talent in fear. Or we can get unbalanced and multiply our talents.

The point is simple.

Don't make balance your goal. If you try, you'll never do anything. You'll be like the person standing on one foot trying to hold up the weight of the world. Instead, in your quiet moments invest time with God authoring your OPUS. This OPUS will keep you centered as you step into unbalance and take action.

Remember, when you prepare for the moment, the moment is prepared for you. Eternity begins now, in this moment. And if you want your time to count, you must count your time.

Day 30 Key Concept: Rediscover balance by returning back to your center of gravity — your OPUS.

A Next Step:

What are your God-given talents? To figure it out, it's often helpful to ask yourself the following questions: What comes easily to you? What do you enjoy doing? What do others often compliment you on? Once you've narrowed it down, take the time to pray and ask God how He wants you to steward your talents? How could your abilities be used for the Kingdom?

_____

_____

_____

_____

_____

_____

_____

_____

_____

_____

_____

_____

_____

_____

_____

_____

_____

APPENDIX

"Everyday"

– Lisa C.

It's time.
Time to celebrate.
Time to love.

My life with you…
Difficult to describe.
Intense,
Ever changing,
Loving,
Fighting,
Growing,
Enduring.

"The first years are the hardest!"
Hang in there.

Hold on.
It's hard.

Not prepared.
Hard consequences.
Finding fault.
Extra-emotional.
Unemotional.

Can this work?

Mentally strong,
Physically tough.
The heart works the hardest,
But our hearts beat
Differently.
Struggling to connect,
Longing for unity,
Broken souls try.
Need to fix the cracks,
Can't fix each other.
Want to find a way
The way to peace
With each other
For each other.
Sometime it feels possible.
Other times it's so far
Away.

Pulled in every direction.
Loyal to our loves,
Responsibility wins.
Finding true joy

Takes a back seat
again.
Yearning for spontaneity
Living to feel loved.
Never enough.
Better together,
Living apart,
The future is unknown.

Complex minds and
Hearts.
Can't hear the words.
Loud, competing voices
Telling us who we are
And what is best for us?
Our hearts whisper soft
And quiet,
Straining to hear the words,
Drowning out the distractions,
Always pulling us away.
Learning to fight back
And not let it wash us
Away.

It is a choice.

The most important
Choice.
To love anyway.
And to you, my darling
I say,
I love you.
I love you.

I love you anyway.
You are the man I
Choose.

Everyday.

NOTES

1. Dave Ramsey. "Separate Checking Accounts are Dangerous." Accessed December 1, 2018, https://www.daveramsey.com/askdave/marriage/separate-checking-accounts-are-dangerous.
2. Art Rainer. The Marriage Challenge: A Finance Guide for Married Couples. (Nashville: B&H Publishing, 2018).
3. Ibid.
4. Jan Karon. In This Mountain. (New York: Viking Publishing, 2002), 260-261.
5. Ibid.

ALSO BY
DEAN FULKS

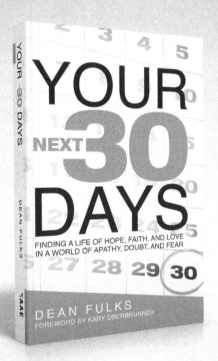

Got a story inside you?

Author Academy Elite could be the perfect choice for helping you write, publish, and market your book.

Discover more at:

http://bit.ly/Next30Days

CPSIA information can be obtained
at www.ICGtesting.com
Printed in the USA
LVHW041130110219
607122LV00001B/1